INSIGHT POCKET GUIDES

Los angeles
& SURROUNDINGS

D0610338

APA PUBLICATIONS
Part of the Langenscheidt Publishing Group

L

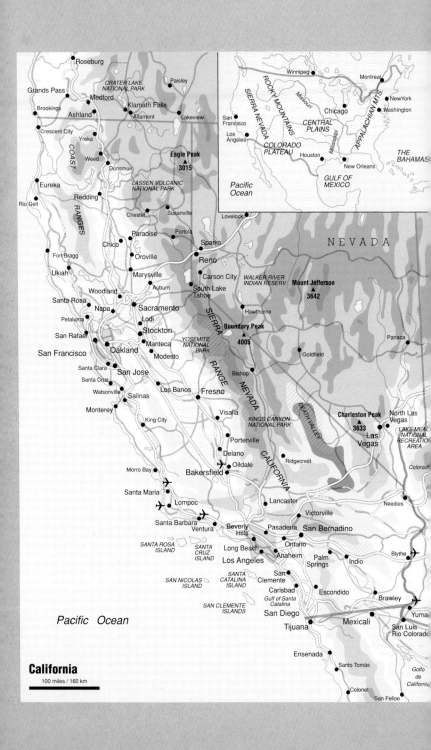

California

100 miles / 160 km

Welcome!

One of the things visitors like most about Southern California is that the people are amiable. It's not unusual for a bus driver or some other stranger to extend a greeting without any ulterior motive; the good weather must have something to do with it. In this way, Los Angeles resembles not so much the enormous city it is but an easygoing middle-American community. Yet Los Angeles plays a big part in the dream-fantasies of all those people who seek to begin a new life.

In these pages, Insight's specialist on California, John Wilcock, has designed four full-day itineraries that take you from Hollywood to LA's downtown to the glittering streets of Beverly Hills. Meal stops are included, as are the beaches of Venice and Malibu. Despite what car-crazy locals might say, it is possible to get around without an automobile, and several of these routes have been designed with pedestrians in mind. For those with a car, however, there is also a (crowd-free) trip around Disneyland, and tours of South Bay, Santa Barbara, Catalina, Palm Springs and San Diego. Supporting these are sections on history and culture, eating out, nightlife and practical information, including hotel listings.

 John Wilcock first discovered California while working as a columnist for New York's *Village Voice*. A number of years later he left the East Coast, settled in California and got to know in earnest the place that had long fascinated him. He thinks you're going to like Los Angeles, but has one word of advice: don't take anything too seriously. It doesn't fit in with the sunshine, the attitude, the whimsical architecture. Much more relaxing is to act like a Californian, and to start each day with a fresh approach.

C O N T E N T S

Pages 2/3:
Union Station,
Los Angeles

Pages 8/9: beauty and the beach

Shopping, Eating Out & Nightlife

Special Events

Practical Information

Maps

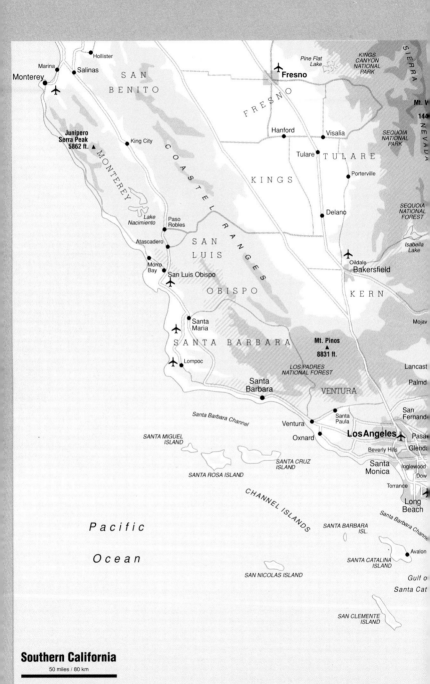

Southern California

50 miles / 80 km

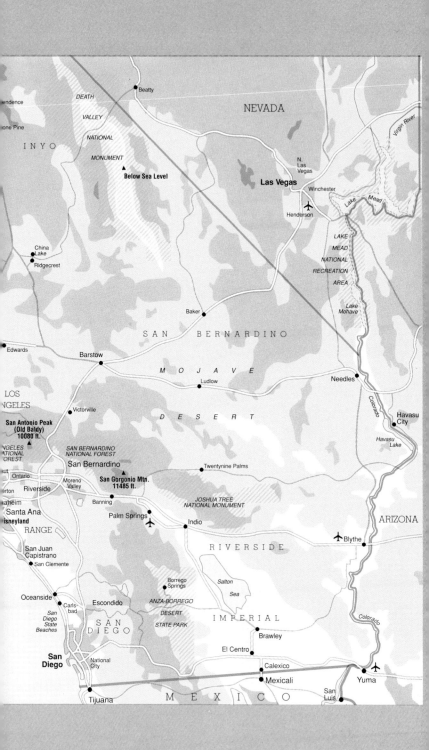

HISTORY &

It was the legend of El Dorado that first brought visitors from distant lands to Southern California, but the early explorers found little of interest. Anchored off the island of Catalina in 1542, the Spanish explorer Juan Rodriguez Cabrillo made friendly contact onshore with the resident Indians to whom he gave beads and other trinkets. Sixty years later, Sebastian Vizcaino, making similar contact, reported that the natives, who lived in rush-covered houses large enough for 50 inhabitants, fished from large canoes fashioned from boards, with an oarsman at each side and a boy in the center to bail out the water.

Neither of these reports did enough to encourage further exploration until 1769, when Gaspar de Portola arrived overland from Baja, California in the south with 60 men in a pack train. Along with the Jesuit padre Junipero Serra, who founded a chain of coastal missions, Portola left the camp at San Diego to open up a

Native American basket maker

Culture

land route to the port of Monterey. In the 10 days before heading north, however, he and his party gave a name to the river, *Rio de Nuestra Señora la Reina de los Angeles de Porciuncula;* discovered the prehistoric tar pits of La Brea; and explored the coastal mountains and the Sepulveda Pass as far away as Lake Encino.

In 1781, as the War of Independence was ending in the east, Felipe de Neve, governor of Spanish California, founded the pueblo of Los Angeles beside the river with 44 settlers from Sonora in northern Mexico. In 1790, the year of the first US census, the pueblo's population was 141, of whom 80 were under 16. Much of LA's subsequent half-century is unrecorded because California's provincial archives were destroyed in the 1850s, but it is known there were few visitors to a city 20 miles inland in the era when most traffic was by sea.

Father Junipero Serra

The 1820s fight by Mexico for independence from Spain scarcely affected Alta ('Upper') California except that Spanish ships no longer had exclusive rights to trade along the coast. As a result, American and British ships also arrived to buy the beef, hides and tallow rendered from the vast herds; in return, ranchers purchased all the needles, boots and other commodities the community badly needed. Los Angeles was still a sleepy place, described in 1841 by an English visitor, Sir George Simpson, as the abode of 'the lowest drunkers and gamblers in the country.' The following year, the discovery of gold at San Fernando brought a sudden influx of swaggering newcomers.

Newcomers Move In

Non-Spaniards had begun to infiltrate the region even before 1846 when, during James K Polk's presidency, an American force under Commodore Robert E Stockton arrived and ran up the American flag. After a temporary setback their occupancy was confirmed and a peace treaty with Mexico was signed in 1848, the same year that gold was discovered 400 miles north at Sutters Mill. This prompted

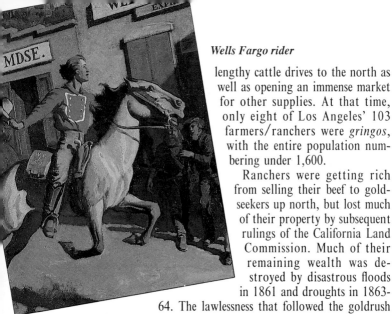

lengthy cattle drives to the north as well as opening an immense market for other supplies. At that time, only eight of Los Angeles' 103 farmers/ranchers were *gringos*, with the entire population numbering under 1,600.

Ranchers were getting rich from selling their beef to gold-seekers up north, but lost much of their property by subsequent rulings of the California Land Commission. Much of their remaining wealth was destroyed by disastrous floods in 1861 and droughts in 1863-64. The lawlessness that followed the goldrush turned LA into what one writer described as 'the toughest town of the entire nation' with the 'greatest number of fights, murders, lynchings and robberies.'

The population of the region was still predominantly Mexican-born, a situation that continued until the 1870s when, sparked by the arrival of the transcontinental railroads, landbooms brought in hundreds of thousands of Anglo-Americans and European immigrants. At the turn of the new century came a rapid growth in transportation, agriculture and light industry attended by lowpaid labor from south of the border. (The Chicano Movement in the late 1960s and '70s gave new stature to Latinos who by the 1980s had regained their ranking as the city's majority population group.)

Natives

Most of the Indians, who as part of the early mission community had been enslaved in an endless round of work and prayer, became laborers and ranch hands as the missions closed. Exposure to disease, alcohol, exploitation and white man's laws almost made them extinct. Mining wastes polluted their salmon streams, forests were cut down for lumber and seven million acres of their land was confiscated. More examples of white racism emerged in 1871, as growing unemployment among whites led to attacks on Asians for

Carving of Native American

'taking all the jobs.' After an incident in which a policeman was killed, rampaging whites lynched 19 people in Chinatown.

The decade that followed saw the phenomenal development of the state's orange industry, centered around Riverside and 13,000 acres of the state's six southern counties. But there were many new claims on the available land, much of which fell into the hands of 'merchants, bankers, professionals and entrepreneurs... the new visionaries – eastern go-getters who brought expansive plans for building fortunes,' as one historian noted. A cabal of railroad magnates ('the Octopus') called the shots, demanding expensive concessions in return for connecting the city to the transcontinental routes. Once the hub had been established, the tracks branched across the state in all directions in a pattern subsequently followed by the freeways.

In the 1880s, Los Angeles battled Southern Pacific and its persuasive owner Collis P Huntington for a port at San Pedro (which already had a wharf built by Phineas Banning to serve the customers of his stagecoach lines), rather than at Santa Monica where SP owned the land and had built a pier. The dispute was not resolved until 1899 when work started on the new harbor at San Pedro. Southern Pacific's other rival, the Santa Fe Railroad, joined it in a fare-cutting war that, along with an aggressive real-estate boom, brought newcomers by the thousands. Across the bay from San Diego trainloads of chic vacationers were building a worldwide reputation for the fabulous Hotel del Coronado.

As visitors bought up land – often from unscrupulous promoters – and took up residence, they spread the word of this idyllic state where almost anything would grow in a climate they likened to that of the cool, balmy Mediterranean.

Striking It Rich

In 1892, two decades after an earlier oil boom had fizzled, Edward Doheny drilled a gusher yielding a modest seven barrels a day near LA's present-day MacArthur Park, an area which within a couple of years became a greasy gulch with wells 'as thick as holes in a pepper pot'. Hundreds of fortunes were made. Oil-fired engines began hauling Santa Fe trains, oil-generated electricity drove the Big Red Cars of the Pacific Electric Railroad's 11,000-mile transportation system. All this occurred before the automobile boom which in the next few decades resulted in 450-square miles being blanketed with freeways, airports, factories, oil refineries, subdivisions, shopping centers, movie studios and industry of all kinds. 'A completely

Cow Boy Throwing Lariat.

motorized civilization,' was how one observer described Southern California in 1927.

By this time, according to social chronicler Louis Adamic, religion had become LA's third activity, ranked just after real estate and movies. Perhaps he was pondering the huge popularity of Aimee Semple McPherson, the first radio evangelist, who was being emulated by a host of other freelance preachers. Undoubtedly, this was the genesis of the city's sometimes deserved reputation as a haven for cults and crazies.

But at least as important as oil, especially to LA, was water, or more particularly the lack of it. Even at the turn of the century it was obvious that growth was going to be stymied unless an adequate supply could be found. Enter the city's visionary water superintendent William Mulholland, with an ambitious plan to bring water from the Owens Valley. The valley was located 250 miles away across the mountains, but by 1913 the project was completed on time and under budget. It was also to the great financial reward of a secret group of investors, who acquired much of the San Fernando Valley land that was to benefit most from the improved water possibilities.

Movies Move In

Around the turn of the century, the movie industry began to blossom as more and more filmmakers from the east were lured to Southern California by a salubrious climate and, more importantly, the distance from the enforcers of Edison's Movie Trust whose stranglehold on patents was hobbling development. By 1910, just as director D W Griffith arrived with 16-year-old Mary Pickford, *The Times* newspaper observed: 'Most movies in America are produced in Los Angeles.'

The rise of the cinema industry was phenomenal. In 1930, four years after a second-string studio, Warner Brothers, took a chance on sound, studio bosses and some top stars were earning $10,000 a week. Greta Garbo was receiving 90,000 fan letters a month, and the industry was among America's top ten moneymakers. Movies and automobiles came together in 1934 with the appearance of the first drive-in movie theater followed, inevitably, by drive-in banks and drive-in restaurants. In 1940 a freeway opened, connecting downtown LA to Pasadena whose annual Tournament of Roses had already celebrated its half-centenary.

Twenty years earlier, LA's population (575,480) had passed that of San Francisco and it was to double again for each of the next three decades, making it by 1950 the country's third largest city. 'Los Angeles lives in the present and dreams of its future,' wrote historian Oliver Carlson. 'San Francisco lives in the present but dreams of its past.'

For much of the first part of this century LA had been regarded as a corrupt, vice-ridden place where too many crooks, cops and politicians were joined in unholy alliance. Raymond Chandler's novels reflected this. 'Law is where you buy it in this town,' he reflected in *Farewell My Lovely*. A 1937 grand jury member reported that LA was rife with 200 gambling dens, 600 whorehouses and 1,800 bookmakers. Something needed to be done.

Four-term mayor Fletcher Bowron presided over some major improvements in the 1940s, expelling the racketeers, helping to initiate the freeway system and the international airport, modernizing the building codes and restricting wanton bulldozing in the hills. His successor Norris Poulson, an early exponent of traffic controls, exchanged his official limousine for a small car and accused Detroit's automakers of putting profit ahead of reducing smog. During Poulson's mayoralty, the long-standing law restricting buildings to 13 stories (150ft), the major reason for the city's sprawl, was repealed. Earthquakes were still expected (and feared), but architects had now devised safeguards.

Winds of Change

Southern California continued to be a magnet for newcomers from all over America, with growth continuing unabated throughout the 1950s, '60s and '70s. Now there was a new element: thousands of

California dreamin'

immigrants fleeing strife and poverty in Asia and Central and South America supplemented the hundreds of thousands of them crossing the Mexican border both legally and illegally. There was not enough work to support them all, a fact which has become increasingly evident with the cutbacks and closings of recent years. The ensuing discontent and frustration was clearly evident long before the so-called Watts Riots of 1965, when a minor police confrontation sparked four days of rioting in the predominantly black area during which 34 people were killed and $40 million worth of property was damaged.

Twenty-five years later, despite 14 years of rule by a black mayor, Tom Bradley, little had changed in the Watts, South Central and the (mainly Latino) East Los Angeles areas. Unemployment levels were astronomic, bankers were still making bad loans to foreign countries but ignoring urban areas of America, complaints of police brutality against minorities were costing the city millions of dollars in legal settlements and racism was endemic. Just as before, the sprawling city was segregated by the distance between its far-flung neighborhoods. In 1992, after a suburban jury had declared four police officers not guilty of unlawfully beating a black motorist - an apparently clear-cut incident seen by television viewers throughout the world - the city exploded yet again with arson, looting, destruction and deaths that exceeded even the earlier uprising. More than 50 people were killed.

As the clean-up continued and the conciliatory talks began yet again, an observer commented: 'They say Los Angeles is usually the first spot where things happen and no doubt it's true this time, too. Unless we do something about the inequalities in our society, there'll be many more incidents like this, in many more places.'

Southern California's strength has always been in its ability to adapt - to a shifting population, to its increased fortunes and to its hard times. This adaptability will hopefully result in a solution to its current problems, for the dream of every Californian is and has always been of a bright and cheerful future.

Historical Highlights

1769 Discovering the Indian village of Yong-na, explorers and missionaries under Captain Gaspar de Portola rename it Porciuncula.

1781 Don Felipe de Neve marches from the San Gabriel mission with 11 Mexican families and discovers Los Angeles.

1790 The community's first census reports that 70 families are living in a total of 30 adobe dwellings.

1842 Gold is discovered near the San Fernando mission.

1846 Start of the US/Mexican War.

1850 On September 9, with a constitution already in place, California becomes the 31st state.

1850s Under successive treaties with the Federal government (never ratified by the Senate) native Indian tribes sign away 90% of the 7½ million acres to which they had legitimate claims.

1858 The Butterfield Stage Line delivers LA's first overland mail.

1867 Gas lamps are installed to illuminate Los Angeles streets.

1874 First navel oranges trees planted at Riverside.

1876 Southern Pacific Railway arrives, nine years before the Santa Fe. Subsequent fare wars greatly boosts the real estate industry.

1887 Horace H Wilcox opens a real estate subdivision that his wife Daieda names Hollywood.

1893 Oil is discovered near what is today's MacArthur Park.

1897 First orchestra west of the Rockies is founded.

1905 Kinney opens his Venetian-style resort near Santa Monica.

1908 Ex-Chicago filmmaker William Selig completes *The Count of Monte Cristo*, LA's first commercial film.

1910 The Flying A Studios sets up shop in Santa Barbara, producing the first of 1,200 films.

1911 Hollywood's first movie, *The Law of the Range*, is filmed in a former tavern at Sunset & Gower.

1913 William Mulholland brings water from the Owens Valley under a $23 million bond issue that has hidden benefits for a secret group of investors.

1926 Second-string studio Warners adds sound to its feature *Don Juan* and the following year gives Al Jolson some dialog in *The Jazz Singer*.

1932 Olympic Games held in world's largest stadium, the LA Coliseum.

1933 Earthquake (6.3 on Richter scale) kills 120 in Los Angeles.

1939 Union Station, last of the great railroad terminals, opens.

1943 Zoot suit riots as sailors and Latinos clash in coastal beach communities.

1946 "Let's not rent out our streets" pleads the *Times* as parking meters are introduced to city thoroughfares.

1947 California legislature passes a law against smog.

1952 Alien Land Act which had denied land ownership to Orientals was declared unconstitutional.

1955 Opening of Disneyland.

1959 Citizens group saves Watts Towers from the wrecking ball.

1963 California's population becomes the largest of all the states.

1965 Watts Riots kill 34 people.

1968 Robert Kennedy assassinated at LA's Ambassador Hotel.

1978 Arsonist sets fire which destroys 160 Malibu homes.

1992 The acquittal of several LA police officers, charged with beating a black motorist, starts riots which kill 51 people.

1994 Earthquake measuring 6.6 in the San Fernando Valley kills 44 people in the LA area.

1998 Getty Center opens to great fanfare, giving LA the cultural lead over San Francisco.

2000 Renovations and new attractions in Downtown and the Hollywood and Vine area ensure the visitors keep coming.

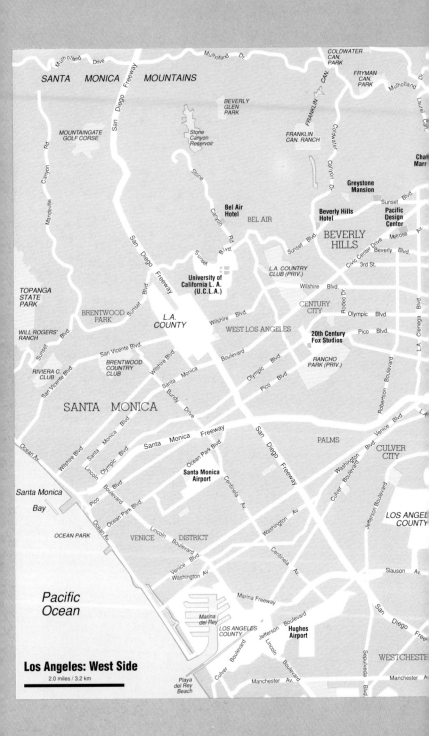

Los Angeles: West Side

2.0 miles / 3.2 km

Day itin

DAY 1

Hollywood

On your first day in LA, we'll take a leisurely stroll through Hollywood, relax in Wattles Park and end the day with drinks or dinner in the starry hills overlooking the city.

—Before setting out (optional): Make a reservation with Graveline Tours (Tel: 816-333 2577); book for dinner at the Yamashiro (Tel: 213-466 5125). Wear comfortable shoes—

Movie-making began in the Los Angeles area very early in the century, but the first studio actually to open in Hollywood was that of the Nestor Film Company which moved into an abandoned tavern (Hollywood, then a separate city, had gone 'dry') on the northwest corner of **Sunset and Gower**, now occupied by the CBS television building. This neighborhood, where we begin our tour, is full of movie memories. On the opposite corner, Channel 5 stands on the site where Warner Bros revolutionized the fledgling industry by having Al Jolson speak in *The Jazz Singer*. And the shopping center called **Gower Gulch** with its hokey, frontier-era signs is a memorial to all the low-budget Western movies that were churned out in the area. The walls of Denny's, one of a moderately-priced

restaurant chain popular with families, are lined with movie posters from that era. It's a good place for breakfast, or for a snack if you're taking the first day easy. The Hollywood Palladium, in the next block, opened in 1940 with Tommy

Hooray for Hollywood

Dorsey's band featuring its young singer Frank Sinatra; across the street, the Earl Carroll Theater was known for its sign: 'Through these portals pass the most beautiful girls in the world,' a reference to the 60 dancers who performed on what was then the world's biggest revolving stage. In the 1960s, as the **Aquarius Theater**, it hosted *Hair* for a record-breaking run.

The distinctive **Cinerama Dome**, the only one in the world made from cement blocks, is the focal point of a glitzy Hollywood marketplace containing shops, open-air restaurants and a multiplex. It was designed by Jon Jerde and his partners who created the exciting Universal CityWalk.

You might want to note the pub-like **Cat & Fiddle**, 6530 Sunset, where you can sit in the pleasant open-air patio with a drink and something English like fish and chips, bangers and mash or shepherd's pie. This is a young hangout with everybody informally dressed in tee shirts and jeans or skirts and sweaters, and everybody chattering away like mad. If you can't make it here for lunch, you might want to keep this place in mind for some early evening when the crowd is at its most interesting.

Angelyne, billboard star of Hollywood

Continue on Sunset until the whimsical **Crossroads of the World**, Hollywood's first shopping center, comes into view and turn down Cherokee on the left, past the post office to **De Longpre Park**. Paul De Longpre, a French-born artist, was the owner of a beautiful mansion and flower-filled garden which was Hollywood's major tourist attraction in the day before the movies arrived. The tiny park that today bears his name is the most peaceful spot around here. Unobtrusively in one corner sits a bust and a statue of Rudolph Valentino, a tribute from his admirers.

Note the fountain at the corner of **Sunset and Vine**, and beside it a plaque claiming that the 1913 production of The *Squaw Man* was filmed here by Cecil B De Mille and Jesse Lasky. Their studio, a big yellow barn, has been carefully preserved and moved to a new location near the Hollywood Bowl. Movie buffs can visit the studio later in the day if they're not tired.

Some of the distinctive 2,518 brass-and-coral terrazzo tiles of the **Walk of Fame**, which begin on Vine, continue all the way up to and then along Hollywood Boulevard. Ever since the first eight stars (Joanne Woodward, Burt Lancaster, Ronald Coleman, Olive Borden, Edward Sedgwick, Ernst Torrence, Preston Foster, Louise Fazenda) were named in 1958, all but about 200 tiles have been filled. At the rate of about one new dedication per month, those should suffice for the next few years.

Street of stars

Barbra Streisand is said to be one of the stars who failed to make the obligatory appearance at a dedication ceremony, although it's presumed that she or her agent paid the usual fee of around $4000 to be listed. Nominations for future listees can be submitted to the Hollywood Historic Trust, 6255 Sunset, Suite 911, LA 90028, which is the same address that issues dates of future ceremonies.

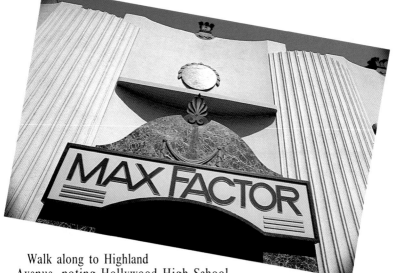

Walk along to Highland Avenue, noting Hollywood High School from which many future stars graduated (including Lana Turner who was discovered in the nearby but long-gone Top Hat café). On Highland we pass the Art Deco **Max Factor building** (*above*) which has been transformed into the **Hollywood History Museum** with four floors of exhibits and displays including costumes and props from old movies. At the corner of Hollywood and Highland opposite the **Hollywood Roosevelt Hotel**, D.W. Griffith's massive *Intolerance* set is being recreated in the new multimillion dollar **entertainment complex** whose centerpiece when it is completed in 2000 will be a 3,300-seat auditorium to house the Academy Awards. The delightful Roosevelt, with its palm-shaded swimming pool and mezzanine filled with early Hollywoodiana (including Disney's first 1931 technicolor camera) was the site of the first public Oscars in 1929.

The hotel is one of the 46 landmarks where Historic Signs are being installed for a do-it-yourself tour along the boulevard (and down Vine), a free list that can be picked up (along with reams of other literature) in the Hollywood Chamber of Commerce office at 7018 Hollywood Boulevard. And if you enjoy movies and TV shows actually being filmed on location, you might want to drop by the Film Permit Office on the 5th floor of 7083 Hollywood Boulevard (Tel: 323-957 1000) to pick up a list of what's scheduled for that particular day.

The **Hollywood Entertainment Museum** (its *Cheers* bar has become a venue for parties) is also along here; so is the restored (by Disney) **El Capitan Theater**, and the **Egyptian Theater**, which is now the headquarters of the **American Cinematheque** dedicated to showing old Hollywood classics as well as interesting films from all over the world. The Egyptian, built right after the worldwide attention given to the discovery of King Tut's tomb and which hosted Hollywood's first movie premiere, *Robin Hood*, in 1922, was the work of the architectural team of Meyer & Holler, as was the nearby **Security Pacific Building** (whose green tower is familiar from TV's *Superman* series). The architects became even more

El Capitan Theater

renowned four years later with the knock-out **Chinese Theater.** This opened with Cecil B DeMille's *King of Kings* at a time when a variety show was also part of the program and nudes were allowed on stage as long as they didn't move.

The forecourt of the Chinese Theater is always crammed with tourists comparing their footprints and handprints with those of such early stars as Pola Negri, Harold Lloyd and William Powell from the 1920s and '30s to Clint Eastwood's 1984 'You Make My Day' sign-off. Children can step into the footprints of Margaret O'Brien and Shirley Temple, and two indented horseshoes left by Gene Autry's mount await any visiting equines. Among tours starting from the Chinese Theater are the infamous **Graveline Tours** ('covers 30 miles of movieland morbidity,' daily at 10am) which visit many of the places where such stars as Humphrey Bogart and gangster Bugsy Siegel came to an untimely end.

A couple of other things are worth noting along this stretch of Hollywood Boulevard: the **Hollywood Wax Museum**, next to what was once the Montmartre Café in which the 1930s stars hung out; **Larry Edmunds bookstore**, #6644, where you can browse for hours among a vast collection of books, posters, pictures and memorabilia about this town's major industry; the tackily irresistible souvenir store **Frederick's of Hollywood** at #6608; and **Musso & Frank's**, the 1916 restaurant that was a haunt of such writers as Nathaniel West, William Faulkner, Raymond Chandler and Robert Benchley. M & F's looks almost unchanged today with its funky old leather booths, but a more cheerful spot for lunch is the aforementioned Cat & Fiddle, a couple of blocks to the east on Sunset. If you didn't take the Graveline Tour we still have time to drop into the public library on Ivar, between Hollywood and Sunset to pore over dozens of books about the movies and their stars, watched over in the comfortable reading room by giant posters advertising silent movies.

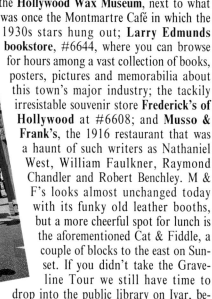

Chinese Theater

Back to Highland up which, about 8 blocks north (bus route MTA420) is the 20,000-seat **Hollywood Bowl**, which hosts concerts most nights from spring through fall. There's a small museum open Tuesday–Saturday 10am–4.30pm. On your way up Highland, watch for the splendid American Legion building to the left and across the street an interesting Moorish courtyard with tower called **Roman Gardens**. Just before the Bowl is a big parking lot, at one end of which is the original yellow barn in which Cecil B De Mille began his career. It's now the **Hollywood Heritage Museum** (Tel: 323-874 2276; open weekends only) and is devoted to the silent picture era.

Behind the barn, Milner Avenue ascends steeply to **Whitley Heights**, an area that once rivaled Beverly Hills as a popular place for stars to live. You might find the hilly terrain too exhausting without a car and nobody is keen to identify for you the former homes of such luminaries as Gloria Swanson, Bette Davis, Rosalind Russell and Rudolph Valentino. Today's residents value their privacy but give their grudging assent to occasional tours by the local civic association.

Alternatively, half a mile west of Highland (MTA buses 1 or 217 along Hollywood Boulevard) a steep walk up Curson brings you to **Wattles Park**. Relatively unvisited, the palm-filled park with its terraced **Japanese garden** stretches all the way up the hillside adjoining Runyon Canyon, now undeveloped (but privately owned) land. Part of the **Santa Monica mountain range**, the park's panoramic views improve as you climb higher, with the best observation point at the crest, almost 1,000ft above sea level.

In the late afternoon, we'll walk back east on Franklin about 6 blocks to Sycamore. Here on the hillside are two astonishing sights: the extraordinary **Magic Castle**, a turreted Victorian-style house above Franklin which restricts admission to magician members or their guests, and further up the hill, a 600-year-old pagoda brought from Japan in 1913 to accompany a traditional Japanese mansion which now serves as the **Yamashiro restaurant**. It's worth the climb to see the view. Even if you don't book for dinner, hang around for a drink on the terrace until dusk, watching the lights of Hollywood go on.

Yamashiro restaurant

DAY 2

Downtown to Venice

Make an early start with a visit to the flower market, followed by breakfast at the 24-hour Original Pantry. Inspect the oldest part of LA as well as the newest skyscrapers and plazas. Have lunch overlooking the sea, then stroll along Venice's boardwalk and canals.

–Before setting out: Reserve for dinner at DC3 at the Santa Monica airport, Tel: 310-399 2323–

We have a busy schedule today and must arise early if we want to observe the activity at the colorful **Flower Market** (7th and Wall streets), which is overflowing with exotic, desert and urban blooms. If you're driving a car, street parking is freely available (and free) before 8am but after leaving the flower market drive half a dozen blocks along 7th Street and left to 877 Figueroa and park in a lot located opposite the **Original Pantry** (our breakfast place) where you can leave your car all day long. For anyone on foot, take the inexpensive DASH bus along 7th. It operates every few minutes in the downtown area from 6.30am on weekdays, from 10am on Saturday. Be sure to pick up a schedule before getting off the bus.

Home Savings Building

Leaving the unpretentious Pantry, which claims to have been open every day for almost 70 years, we walk up Figueroa, past the **Seventh Street Market Plaza**, a stylish mall whose sunken plaza with its open-air restaurant sits among three-story palm trees shading such stalwart stores as Bullocks, Benetton and the May Company. Scattered around the plaza are several art works, including a bronze businessman with head bent, located on the north side of the Citicorp Center.

Cross the street and walk half a block to the **Fine Arts Building** at 811 West 7th, its artists' studios long converted to offices. A

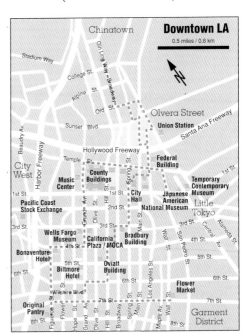

Wells Fargo wagon

medieval-style lobby with 15 chandeliers and a tiled fountain, hosts color drawings of some of the ambitious art works planned for stations of the city's new Metro system.

Admire the gaudy, gilded, façade of the **Home Savings Building** as you head back to Figueroa. The stepped, white tower of the **777 Building** ('subtle profiles and strong silhouettes' says one critic) was created by Argentine-born Cesar Pelli, who was also responsible for the Pacific Design Center in West Hollywood. 'In this city… I became an American architect,' he boasts. A subtle fountain by Eric Orr sits outside the **Sanwa Bank** building in the 80-ft high Art Deco lobby in which, among acres of brown marble, sit two of the largest plants ever seen in captivity.

From Arco Plaza across the street, take the escalator into the glitzy **Bonaventure Hotel** with its multi-level lounges and engaging perspectives. Traverse the second-floor bridge into the *other* **Arco Plaza**, heading up past the rocky waterfall and 40-ft palms, then up the stylish Bunker Hill steps. Turn onto Hope and up Grand to the **Wells Fargo Museum** (Monday–Friday 9am–4pm, free). Containing the stagecoaches that tamed the West and made heroes out of cowboys, this museum is a must-see for anyone who holds a romantic view of the Wild West. Heavy art and sculpture by the likes of Rauschenberg, Stella and Mark DiSuvero dot the otherwise uninspiring plaza.

Across the street is MOCA, the **Museum of Contemporary Art**, located in a classy building by Arata Isozaki that has another eye-catching fountain. Grab the DASH bus (DD route on weekends; B on weekdays) which heads north on Grand past the the **Music Center** and the site for Frank Gehry's long-delayed Disney Concert Hall at 1st Street and up into shabby **Chinatown**, barely worth a stop. There the bus reverses direction heading down to **Olvera Street**. Pick up a DART map from the bus driver.

Olvera Street features Mexican stalls and a strolling mariachi band that'll serenade us as we sip a frozen margarita (five flavors) under the sidewalk awning of **La**

Golondrina, the city's first brick building (1850). This was home to the Pellenconi family whose piano, a neighborly gift, sits across the street in the older (much restored) **Avila Adobe** (free admission). A statue of Felipe de Neve, California's first governor in 1775 who laid out this pueblo, dominates the plaza across which is the (now empty) Pico House which a century later (and a century ago) was the home of the *last* Spanish governor, Pio Pico. The adjoining **Helman Quon** building, once a Chinese store, is now a Parks Department office offering (free) **morning tours** of this neighborhood. Look in the firehouse for the picture of Blackie, the city's last firehorse.

Cross the busy highway, past the statue of Father Junipero Serra (1713-84), founder of California's earliest missions, and take a look at the still majestic **Union Station** whose leather seats and stratospheric ceiling has been seen in scores of old newsreels: it is nicely maintained by Amtrak which operates about 20 trains a day up the coast, down to the Mexican border and into the desert.

Pause for a coffee at a table in the garden behind Traxx before either reboarding DASH to look around **Little Tokyo** (the spectacular **Japanese America Museum** at 369 First Street; MOCA's adjoining Geffen Contemporary; the **New Otani Hotel**'s fourth floor garden; the **Yaohan Plaza Shopping Center** at Central Avenue and 3rd Street), or walking three blocks down to **City Hall**. Here you can take an elevator to the 22nd floor, then transfer to the Tower Elevator (Tuesday–Friday 10am–2pm). There is a rewarding overview of downtown and the hillside parks to the north.

Behind Joseph Young's **Triforium**, a gaudy sculpture adjoining the sunken plaza below, is the **Children's Museum** where the face-painting, paper-sculpture class, shadow wall, velcro cushion room, bus driver's cab and (stationary) police motor cycle tend to keep kids diverted for an hour or two. Children aren't admitted without adults but an occasional parent has been known to park her children in search of a little quality time of her own.

There's much to see on and around Broadway, two blocks south: the magnificent **Bradbury Building** (1893) whose winding staircase, wrought-iron elevators and rich woodwork have endeared it to moviemakers; the elegant lobby of architect S. Charles Lee's **Los Angeles Theater** (6th Street) which premiered Charles Chaplin's *City Lights* in 1931; and the exciting **Grand Central Market** (all kinds of food, neon signs, lots of life). Exit at the back of the market and take a round trip on the charming **Angels Flight**, built in 1901 to carry residents 335 feet up to the apartments atop Bunker Hill. One of those residents was author Raymond Chandler who mentioned it in his novel *The King in Yellow*. When the tiny funicular was demolished in 1969, the authorities promised it would be rebuilt – a promise that was finally delivered 26 years later. Atop the hill is California Plaza whose delightful fountain-filled **Water Court** is a popular spot for outdoor lunch and the venue for a wide variety of concerts during the long summer.

Further down Hill Street is **Pershing Square**, once historic but now redesigned into a sterile, lifeless plaza. You might like to check out the sumptuous lobby of the **Regal Biltmore Hotel**, one block west, and its near-neighbor the magnificent **Central Library** with garden restaurant nearby.

Walk down to Hope Street and west along 7th Street. The MTA's ambitious plans for subways and light rail routes around the region have been somewhat curbed by opposition from citizen groups who have demanded more transit funds be spent on improving the bus system. Notwithstanding such problems, from the Metro Center at 7th and Flower Streets the Red Line already runs out to Hollywood (and eventually to Universal City) and the Blue Line down to Long Beach.

Olvera Market

But what we'll do today is head a block north from the Metro Center to catch the bus along Wilshire, transferring at Robertson Boulevard in Beverly Hills to MTA220 which runs down to the ocean, passing through Culver City where MGM and Columbia Pictures have their production studios.

At **Marina del Rey**, we debark from the bus outside the charmingly phony **Fisherman's Village** (the 'lighthouse' is a fast-food stand) and choose from several restaurants for lunch. These range from the reasonably-priced El Torito for Mexican fare to Shanghai Red's, which has all the appealing ambience of a century-old inn but has actually been here for only the 30 years since the marina was developed. All the restaurants overlook the harbor, which has berths for 6,000 boats. After lunch we board the northbound Big Blue Bus, alighting at Venice Boulevard to pick up some cookies at the corner liquor

Marina del Rey canal

store. Walk along Venice Boulevard South 1 block and from the bridge turn right to tour the tranquil **Venice canal area**.

Venice's canal system dates from 1905 when tobacco tycoon Abbott Kinney turned his apparently worthless marshland into a small-town replica of Venice, Italy, complete with gondolas, humped bridges, Japanese lanterns and inexpensive homes on lots which have become worth millions of dollars.

The circulating system which was intended to flush the canals with sea water at every tide never worked very well, and over the years the canals have become shallow, polluted and much diminished. But it's still a delightful walk along the canal-side paths to admire the attractive homes and feed the ducks with those cookies you had the foresight to bring.

Our next stop is **Windward Avenue**, 5 blocks to the north. Along this colonnaded block in Kinney's day was the St Mark's Hotel (modeled after the Doge's Palace), popular with the early movie stars who along with most other Angelenos regarded Venice as their playground. Barney Oldfield won the first (and only) Venice Grand Prix back in 1916 and Lawrence Welk played for years at a now-defunct ballroom.

The **Venice boardwalk**, actually a lengthy promenade running all the way up to Santa Monica, is the major attraction today, filled as it is with the kind of people that every town regards as its Bohemian element. Cyclists and skaters race endlessly back and forth, men and women strut around in bizarre costumes, chainsaw jugglers, musicians, fire-eaters, acrobats, runaways and tourists all mingle in an almost endless day and night parade, gathering in groups to watch an impromptu performance or the macho posturings at **Muscle Beach**. There's a childrens' playground here and also bleachers where you can sit.

Muscle Beach

Back on Ocean Avenue, take Big Blue Bus 2 up a few blocks to Ocean Park and transfer to the No 8 bus which runs along the north side of Santa Monica airport. From **Clover Park**, walk a couple of blocks down to the **Museum of Flying** (which closes, alas, at 5pm). It was here, in 1977 at the McDonnell Douglas plant, that the first DC3 airplane was built, and it is here in this setting that we have dinner (California-style cuisine) in the restaurant of the same name.

Barnsdall Park to Beverly Hills

Admire a Frank Lloyd Wright house and the graves of old-time stars; lunch at Farmers Market; visit the La Brea Tar Pits; window shop along glittering Rodeo Drive, then wind up the day with dinner in Santa Monica in the mall or on the pier.

—Before setting out: Call to see when you can tour Hollyhock House (Tel: 323-662 7262). Acquire small change for bus fares. RTD bus information: Tel: 213-626 4455. Prepare for tomorrow by booking a car, and calling the Getty Center (Tel: 310-440 7300, closed Mon) to make a required reservation in the car park—

Among those who thought that the late Frank Lloyd Wright was America's greatest architect was the eccentric oil heiress Aline Barnsdall, who met Wright in Chicago and invited him back to Los Angeles to design a theater for her. **Barnsdall Park** is the 36-acre hilltop lot near the intersection of Hollywood and Sunset boulevards on which in the 1920s he built the Mayan-style **Hollyhock House** with its rooms opening onto several lush and extremely attractive, decorative patios. But Ms Barnsdall wasn't very happy in her new home and shortly afterwards donated it to the city, whose Cultural Affairs department conducts regular tours. We can climb the hill and admire the house from the outside even when there isn't a tour.

After Barnsdall Park, take the MTA204 bus down Vermont, transfer to the MTA4 OR 304 along Santa Monica and alight at Van Ness. Here, through the archway, is the

French poster of 'The Sheik'

Hollywood Memorial Park Cemetery; ask for a free map at the office by the entrance, then take the path to the left. Just past the first avenue is the tomb of Cecil B De Mille. Also here in section 8, is the last resting place of tycoon William Randolph Hearst's mistress Marion Davies close to the grave of Tyrone Power. Flowers grow from the otherwise-simple lakeside plot of actress Virginia Rappe (whose fatal rape at a hotel party in 1921 ended the career

Canter's deli counter

of comic Fatty Arbuckle) and there are flowers, too, flanking the crypt of Rudolph Valentino.

In 1926, when he died at 31, Valentino was the biggest star in the world (*The Sheik, Seven Horsemen of the Apocalypse*) and 10,000 mourners jammed this cemetery for his funeral. Even now, 7 decades after his death, the crypt draws crowds of people. It is set into the interior wall of the Cathedral Mausoleum, the enormous building across from the lake. Next to it is the impressive sunken garden and marble monument (paid for by Mary Pickford, who, curiously, is buried elsewhere), marking the grave of Douglas Fairbanks Sr who died, aged 56, in 1939. Other famous people are buried in this vast graveyard recently acquired by new owners.

Backing on to the cemetery on Melrose is **Paramount Pictures**. Walk down Van Ness to Melrose, where we will see the famous arched entrance to the 62-acre lot from which came films as varied as De Mille's *Cleopatra*, the Crosby/Hope/Lamour *Road* series, and more recently, *Star Trek*. Such top TV series as *Frazier* and *Entertainment Tonight* are filmed at Paramount these days and there is a limited tour program (Tel: 323-950 1777 for information).

We're off for lunch at the **Farmers Market**; to get there we'll take the MTA10 bus along Melrose, noting all the trendy shops with oddball names on and west of La Brea and transferring at Fairfax to the MTA217 running down to 3rd Street. On the way, watch for **Canter's** 24-hour delicatessen on the right; it's where all homesick New Yorkers still line up for pastrami sandwiches.

The market, with its landmark clock tower and more than 100 shops, stalls and restaurants, is a delightful place to dally. Wander the aisles and buy a souvenir, or visit the post office, before choosing your favorite food from one of the counters and sitting down to eat at an outdoor table. Founded by Earl Gilmore during the Depression years, it's the kind of place where you're still likely to see a well-known face, especially as the studios of CBS Television are right next door. If you're in a car, by the way, there's always ample free parking.

After lunch we get back on the Fairfax bus, or walk for about half a mile, down to Wilshire Boulevard, turning left to visit the

Beverly Hills Witches House

County Museum of Art's collection of Old Masters. Personally, I'm more intrigued by the **La Brea Tar Pits** next door. Here, two million years ago, mighty mammoths and dozens of other creatures stopped to drink, lured by a shimmering pool that was to become their grave but which preserved their skeletons to this day. Major Henry Hancock, veteran of the war with Mexico and successful gold prospector, bought this land for $2.50 an acre in the 1860s and became even richer by shipping out most of the asphalt that paved the streets of San Francisco. You'll find the story of the 1905 excavations recounted in the adjoining building.

Back to the MTA20 bus for our next stop, **Beverly Hills**, alighting at famous **Rodeo Drive**. Steps opposite the Regent Beverly Wilshire lead up to **Two Rodeo Drive**, Hollywood's evocation of a chic European street with cobblestones and stratospheric prices. Further up Rodeo are such glitzy shops as Cartier, Hermes and Gucci. Tourism accounts for 40 percent of sales on Rodeo, where rents are around $200 per square foot.

Beverly Hills' shopping area ends where the illuminated fountain marks the intersection of Wilshire and Santa Monica boulevards. Both roads run out to the coast, the latter passing **Century City** – a soulless cluster of high-rent highrises on the site of the old 20th Century Fox lot – and the former passing through **Westwood 'Village.'** There was a time when Westwood actually was a village but for many years now it's been a sort of company town for the University of California whose campus it adjoins. It is a popular venue for young people from other parts of town attending premieres at the

La Brea Tar Pits

many cinemas. On weekend nights it's probably the last place you'd want to be. UCLA, on the other hand, has a pleasant, tree-shaded campus on which there are daily activities.

We leave the campus at the northern end, catching an MTA2 OR 302 bus west along Sunset Boulevard to admire some of the

Two Rodeo Drive

sprawling mansions at this western end. You'll
notice the turn-off to the Will Rogers Ranch on
the right and a couple of miles further, after
passing through Pacific Palisades, the grounds of
the Self Realization Fellowship on the left. We'll
visit both of these on tomorrow's tour, but now
you know where they are.

Sunset Boulevard ends at the coast where we'll
pause to watch the sunset. Then catch the MTA434
which runs from Union Station to Malibu via the 10
freeway. Ride down the Pacific Coast Highway to
Santa Monica Boulevard then walk 3 blocks inland to
Santa Monica Place, a pedestrian mall with shops,
cafés and movie theaters, and an enclosed shopping
center (designed by the local architect Frank Gehry) where dozens
of counters offer any kind of food you can imagine. Alternatively,
you might want to walk back to the beach and have dinner on the
pier. **Santa Monica Pier** is a delightful place for a stroll, with its
amusement arcades, aquarium and century-old carousel.

Hollywood Hills to Malibu

**Get a great view of the famous Hollywood sign and take a rural
drive. Tour Bel Air, the Self Realization Foundation lakeside
shrine, the Will Rogers ranch and the Getty Center. Try an (optional) visit to a nudist colony, and finish the day in Malibu.**

*—We'll need a car for today's route, although bus routes serve three
of the last four attractions. If you plan to visit 'clothes-optional'
Elysium Fields, call first (Tel: 310-455 1000). Make a reservation
at Taverna Tony's (Tel: 310-317 9669) in Malibu—*

As the famous **Hollywood sign** with its 50-ft letters is virtually in-
accessible (except via an exhausting climb through tangled under-
brush from Beachwood Drive), the best view of it is from beside the
Hollywood Reservoir which is itself difficult to reach. Pay careful
attention: drive up Ivar north of Franklin, left on Dix Street, right
on Holly Drive under the freeway, right again on Deep Dell Place
to Weidlake Drive, continue to where it dead-ends outside the
reservoir fence. Joggers are most of the folk we find up here, along
with a few lovers and people walking their dogs. It's 3 miles

around the reservoir but we can drive only partly around it and even then only if we enter from the other side, so to get down to the Hollywood freeway we have to return the way we came.

At the freeway, on Cahuenga Boulevard East which parallels it, we could if we had the time head north to **Mulholland Drive**, an attractive highway that winds around the crest of the Santa Monica mountains for fully 50 miles. Despite being lined in part by magnificent homes, it is so unspoiled that one 7-mile section – between the San Diego freeway and Topanga Canyon – remains (deliberately) unpaved. Needless to say, the views of both Hollywood and the San Fernando Valley are spectacular by day or night. Avoid the unpaved section at night.

The major routes connecting the West Side and the Valley are the various canyon roads that spiral down from Mulholland Drive to Sunset Boulevard. Just west of Beverly Drive beside the **Beverly Hills Hotel** – whose Polo Lounge is still a good place to watch for stars – is Benedict Canyon.

Heading up **Benedict Canyon Drive,** we turn left onto Shadybrook, left again onto Cielo Drive and then head up to **1436 Bella Drive**, a dead end, to look at Rudoph Valentino's old home. The house's name, Falcon's Lair, can still be seen high up on the right side of the gate (which, incidentally, blocks off most of the view).

Back down to Benedict Canyon Drive and first left up Estate Drive to **Tower Grove Drive** at whose junction with **Seabright** is a spectacular view and a spectacular house. It's the same site, but not the same house where silent-screen star John Gilbert and Greta Garbo used to spend lazy afternoons when Gilbert's mansion stood here. Off

Cowboy star Will Rogers

Benedict Canyon further down, just before it meets Sunset, turn left up Summit to see where (at number 1143) **Pickfair**, the mansion of early Hollywood's 'royal' couple Mary Pickford and Douglas Fairbanks, used to stand. Sadly, the micro-talented starlet Pia Zadora and her husband pulled the house down a few years ago.

Beverly Glen crosses Sunset about 1 mile to the west. Many famous people live here, although high walls, gates and shrubberies shield most of the houses from sight. Just beyond the Glen, turn right up Bel Air Road, left along Bellagio and right up Copa de Oro which segues into Stone Canyon. Here we'll stop to look

Aeriel view of the Getty Center

around and possibly have lunch or a drink at the **Bel Air Hotel**, one of the West Coast's most romantic hideaways. It has its own stream complete with swans, and is much preferred by the cognoscenti to its more famous Beverly Hills rival.

At Westwood the 405 freeway crosses Sunset and just to the north you'll see the gleaming, white **Getty Center** perched on a hill. If you haven't made a reservation for the car park you'll be admitted only if you arrive by taxi or bus (MTA561 and Big Blue 14) or take a shuttle from a nearby hotel such as the Brentwood Holiday Inn (Tel: 310-476 6411). An electric tram runs up from the museum car park to pavilions displaying paintings, sculpture, drawings and photographs, and a research center with its 800,000-volume art library. There's also a fascinating garden plus café and restaurant and spectacular, panoramic views from the terrace.

More than a decade in construction at a cost totalling one billion dollars, the 'white city on the hill' with its plazas and fountains has been compared to a medieval castle.

Architect Richard Meier lived much of the time in a rat-infested shack on the rugged, hilltop site which he described as the most beautiful he had ever been invited to build on. In its construction, he said he had tried to strike a balance between the man-made and natural worlds.

The collections are superb, ranging from a chalk drawing by Rem-

View of the entrance hall rotunda

Van Gogh's 'Irises'

brandt to David Hockney's contemporary photographic assemblages, from 16th century Italian furniture to Van Gogh's luminous *Irises*. The Getty collection of more than 100 illuminated manuscripts illustrates the development of this craft between the 10th and 16th centuries.

Back on Sunset, look out for the signposted road after Brentwood which winds round the hill for almost a mile to the parking lot of the **Will Rogers Ranch** (daily 10am–5pm, parking fee). The low-slung home is a delight, furnished in Western style with Navaho baskets and blankets and solid, hand-carved furniture. It's pretty much the way that the beloved cowboy star left it when he died in a 1935 air crash in Alaska. Don't miss the excellent short film about the life of the cowboy turned comic and columnist which runs continuously between 10am and 5pm each day. Polo matches occasionally take place on the grounds which are also a favorite picnic spot. A 2-mile trail leads up into **Topanga State Park**.

Our final stop on Sunset, just before the coast, is to look around the charming lakeside shrine of the **Self Realization Fellowship** with its swans, waterfall, houseboat and windmill church. Watch for the giant lotus archway on the left for the unexpected turn-off. Pull into the parking lot (free) and then walk all the way around the lake. Where Sunset hits the Pacific Coast Highway, you're only about a mile from the old **Getty Museum**, due to reopen in 2001 with the antiquities collection.

The less culturally-inclined might enjoy a visit to **Elysium Fields**, 5 miles up Topanga Canyon whose turnoff is about a mile beyond the museum. Whatever your fantasies might have been about nudist camps, they probably don't resemble the reality of this 'clothes-optional resort' spread over a gently sloping grassy area fringed by tennis and volley ball courts, a large swimming pool, sauna and a bubbling hot tub that holds 24 people. Several masseurs can usually be found at work on the grounds. 'Nude is not lewd' proclaimed the late founder Ed Lange, who created this tranquil hillside park high up in the Santa Monica mountains almost 30 years ago.

Ed claimed that the radical act of going naked changed many

people's lives and more than one person admitted they felt they were shedding their problems as well as their garments. Snacks, towels and tee-shirts are sold in the office, which is where visitors register on arrival. Elysium is a membership club but guests can visit for the day (the price is reasonable) or attend a free 30-minute orientation tour on certain mornings.

Paying visitors may stay at Elysium all day, but when you get hungry you might want to head down to Malibu to eat. Drive back down Topanga Canyon and turn right up the Pacific Coast Highway to Cross Creek. Here, behind the Civic Center, is **Taverna Tony's**, a lively Greek restaurant with music. En route you'll pass the derelict Malibu Pier, which has been closed for years due to storm damage. It was built by Malibu's founder Frederick Rindge just before his death in 1905.

Just north of the pier is the historic **Adamson House**, built in 1929 by May Rindge, his widow. Fortunately it is as attractive outside as inside because if you want to see the interior with its little museum packed with photographs of the early Malibu community you'll have to come back between Wednesday–Saturday 11am–3pm. There's a small admission fee for the tours and a movie is shown depicting Malibu's history.

Even when the house is closed you can drive or walk up to admire the tiled terrace, fountains, bottle-glass windows and well-kept gardens. Frederick Rindge bought hundreds of acres of surrounding land for $10 per acre back in 1887.

Malibu Beach

A display in the museum explains that the real Malibu Gold is real estate: Bing Cros-by's house, worth $8,700 in 1931, was bought for almost $2 million by Robert Redford 50 years on. In 1928 Harold Lloyd's house cost $6,400, but Linda Ronstadt paid $1.3 million in 1985. Entering the 21st century, real estate prices are going through the roof, with only the most lavishly paid people able to afford them.

Huntington House library

The Rose Bowl and Gardens

The lovely Huntington Gardens and the homes of Pasadena make a relaxing afternoon away from the urban sprawl.

—This trip is easier with a car, but MTA buses 401 and 402 from Olive Street downtown run out to Pasadena, where a transfer is made to MTA177 at California Street. Make a reservation for afternoon tea (Tel: 818-683 8131) at the Huntington Gardens. If it's Thursday–Sunday and you begin early enough you might have time to tour the Gamble House (for reservations Tel: 818-793 3334)–

We alight from the bus on California Street at Allen Street after passing the California Institute of Technology. Walk down to Orlando to enter the former gardens and library of multi-millionaire Henry Edwards Huntington, a railroad magnate who with his wife Arabella assembled one of the most important collections of art and rare books in the country. Once past the orange grove, turn slightly right to enter the immense **Huntington Gardens** lined with

17th-century statues and flanked by a garden of camellias (in winter, azaleas). There's another camellia garden over to your far right but first walk through the colorful Shakespeare garden with its bust of the bard and almost all of the flowers mentioned in his works. Then turn left in front of the library and make a brisk tour of the Palm Garden and Desert Garden before crossing back over the main path and heading over past the lily pond.

Because the 15 gardens occupy more than 100 acres, it's easy to find some tranquil spot with nothing but the sound of birds for company. Beyond the lily pond are the Subtropical Garden, the Australian Garden and the Japanese and Zen gardens flanking a delightful 19th-century Japanese house. After crossing the little red bridge over the carp-filled lake and climbing the steps, you'll find yourself in the Rose Garden and just in time for tea (you did make a reservation, didn't you?) at the charming **Rose Garden Room**. The tea room closes at 3.45pm (Wednesday–Sunday), which is why we have wasted no time. We have until 4.30pm to complete our tour.

The most treasures are to be found in the **Huntington Gallery** (the family home from 1850 to 1927), with the main gallery offering several world-famous paintings: Thomas Gainsborough's *Blue Boy* (c 1770); Thomas Lawrence's *Pinkie* (1794); Sir Joshua Reynolds' *Mrs Siddons* (1784); and a landscape by John Constable, *View on the Stour* (1822). The airy building, a pleasure to walk around, is itself something of a work of art and everything in it has significance, from the carpets woven for Louis XIV to the early Wedgwood tureens. Many pictures will look familiar from reproductions, in particular one of the portraits of George Washington, by Gilbert Stuart, in the dining room. Behind the main gallery, back across the Shakespeare Garden, the **Scott Gallery** is devoted to American art showing its development from the English influence in the 18th century to the aptly-named **Twentieth Century Gallery** in which you'll find works by Edward Hopper, John Sloan and other members of the New York group known as the Ashcan School.

Try to save some time for **the library**, which boasts an astonishing four million items. Among those on show are a 1410 edition of Chaucer's *Canterbury Tales*, a Gutenberg Bible, Audubon prints and an early Shakespeare folio as well as a collection of rare 19th-century dime-store novels. Huntington was a world-class collector in the Hearstian mode. One of his letters, written in 1917, refers to the $1 million he had just spent on purchasing the Earl of Ellesmere's library.

The Huntington is open daily except Mondays from 12.30pm, with 90-minute tours of the grounds at 1pm. A 10-minute orientation slide show precedes the tour. Admission is free, under the terms of Huntington's will, but donations are invited. Parking is available for a fee. Our last stop should be at the excellent bookshop which has jigsaw puzzles made from medieval maps, and other esoterica.

Pasadena itself is a fairly commonplace town which comes fully alive once a year during January's **Rose Bowl** football game and the famous Tournament of Roses Parade. If there's still time, get back on the MTA177 and head along California and up Orange Grove. Just before the freeway is the

Huntington Gardens

Norton Simon Museum (Thursday–Sunday, noon–6pm, admission fee, Tel: 818-449 6840) with its world-class collection of Asian and European art. Across the freeway, within walking distance, is the 18-room Freyes Mansion (1905), home of the **Pasadena Historical Museum** (Thurday–Sunday, 1–4pm, admission fee, Tel: 818-571 1660), where D W Griffiths shot one of his first films.

Half a block away is the impressive **Gamble House** (Thursday–Sunday, noon–3pm, reservations essential, Tel: 818-793 3334), built for David Gamble (of Procter & Gamble, America's biggest soap company) in 1908. Technically a California-style 'bungalow,' the terraced, wood-tiled house is a product of the turn-of-the-century Arts and Crafts Movement of which Pasadena's Greene brothers, Charles Sumner and Henry Mather, were noted members. Impressive from the outside (and therefore worth seeing even when closed), its interior is a knockout, but to see this you must reserve a place on one of the 10-member tours.

EXCURSIONS
Disneyland

A no-nonsense guide to the world of Mickey Mouse, with tips on the best attractions and how to make your trip run smoothly.

—You can get to Disneyland by train from LA's Union Station to Fullerton, transferring to an Orange County bus; by MTA460 bus from 6th and Grand streets downtown and on a number of different tours. All-in package tours can be arranged via Walt Disney Travel (Tel: 714-520 5050). For drivers, the route is south along Interstate 5, the Santa Ana freeway. Opening hours are 9am–9pm, until midnight on Saturday. Main Street opens at 8.30am–

'The way I see it, Disneyland will never be finished,' Walt Disney once said. 'I've always wanted to work on something alive, something that keeps growing. We've got that at Disneyland.'

Disneyland seems to grow in size (and crowds) year by year. All advice on how to avoid any built-in problems boils down to com-

Taking a spin at Disneyland

mon sense: avoid summer, Christmas, Thanksgiving, all holidays and weekends if you possibly can, and try to visit on a midweek day. Arrive before opening time, so you have already inspected Main Street and worked out your schedule from the map by the time the rest of the park opens half an hour later.

To avoid having to back-track, the best strategy is to cover the park logically, dealing with one 'land' at a time. As two of the most popular rides – **Astro Orbitor** and **Rocket Rods** – are both in **Tomorrowland**, place yourself at the top of Main Street so you can zip right in there (maybe from the back door of a shop), as soon as it's allowed. Both rides, incidentally, are the white-knuckle kind and not for the faint-hearted. Currently the park's most popular ride is **Indiana Jones** in **Adventureland**.

Mad Hatter's Tea Party

The other 'rules' for Disneyland are equally simple: eat at unconventional times to bypass crowds as much as possible, return to your hotel for an afternoon rest or swim so you can continue refreshed later in the day, and study the daily schedule to see what times large numbers will be siphoned off watching some special event. In this way you can avoid making lines even longer, and slip in quickly yourself.

From the beginning, Disney planners were constantly seeking new ways to keep those waiting in line diverted. Walt Disney, living for long periods of time in a private apartment above the fire station on Main Street, was always wandering around watching lines to devise better ways of crowd control

Because **Main Street** opens earlier, closes later and has no rides, it can be a very flexible destination. It's also the place to get good information and maps (**City Hall**), exchange foreign currency and get credit card advances (Bank of Main Street), rent a camera or camcorder (Kodak Camera Center), hire a stroller or wheelchair (just inside the main entrance), stash your surplus items in a handy locker (adjoining Disney Clothiers) and attend to your infant in the Baby Center.

The 15-minute **Great Moments With Mr Lincoln** show and the silent cartoon program at the **Cinema**, being almost always uncrowded, are nice, cool places to take the weight off your feet; and the **Penny Arcade** is the cheapest entertainment in the entire park. Don't rush to take the 18-minute **railroad circuit**: best to wait un-

Frontierland

til it fits conveniently into your schedule. But don't miss it either; the train's passage through the Grand Canyon is charming. Lines are shortest at the **Mickey's Toontown station**, except of course when the nighttime disco is operating.

Fantasyland is probably the kids' favorite, but some of the rides there, such as **Peter Pan's Flight, Mr Toad's Wild Ride, Alice in Wonderland** and **Snow White's Scary Adventure**, seem to be aimed as much at adults as children. The first two are especially interesting, demonstrating how much illusion owes to darkness and luminous paint.

In sharp contrast is that old favorite, **It's A Small World**, which first emerged as a Disney-created attraction on behalf of Pepsi-Cola and UNICEF in the 1964 New York World's Fair. It's a delightfully ageless attraction not to be missed, and certainly among the handful that can be enjoyed over and over again. Out of Disney's New York World's Fair experiences grew the concept of 'editing' most rides by pointing the car (oval-shaped pods from which the passenger could see only ahead) at a specific scene, then cutting to another scene by spinning the car suddenly to left or right.

Everybody, of course, admires and usually rides to, from or around the 147-ft **Matterhorn** – the real thing is 100 times larger. When its 500-ton steel framework was first erected, it was built from the top down to stop the subsequent cement droppings spoiling the appearance of the slopes below.

From the **Sleeping Beauty Castle** and the steam train to the Mark Twain Steamboat, most structures in Disneyland are scaled down versions of their originals. Movie set designers were experts at using tricks of scale to make buildings seem taller or further away. The first floor of buildings on Main Street, for example, is 90 percent of full size, the second floor 80 percent and so on.

How much time you have available will dictate the rest of your itinerary, but definitely visit **New Orleans Square** with its nearby **Pirates of the Caribbean** and **Haunted Mansion**, indisputably among the top attractions, as is **Honey,**

Disney witch

I Shrunk the Audience. Also try not to miss the amusingly hokey **Big Thunder Mountain Railroad**.

Live animals, whose involvement has now been abandoned altogether, were always harder to deal with than mechanical versions. But the science of audi-animatronics which came out of research for America's Space Program, resulted not only in the lifelike Abraham Lincoln, but the triumph of the 225 talking birds and flowers of the **Enchanted Tiki Room**. Lincoln himself had been planned as but one element in a Hall of Presidents along a Liberty Street which was never built. One of Disney's newer attractions, **Innoventions**, in Tomorrowland, is a melange of games and technological experiences inside a circular moving building.

Both the **Jungle Cruise** and the **Mark Twain Steamboat** are fun, and the nighttime spectacular **Fantasmic** is so outstanding that spectators start positioning themselves 2 hours before it begins (so get in there). Between the ingenious **Swiss Family Treehouse** (worth inspecting) and the **Rivers of America**, on which the nightly fireworks extravaganza takes place, is one of the most under-estimated attractions in the park, the upstairs **Disney Gallery**, in pseudo-Southern mansion style. Off a tranquil patio with a fountain are rooms lined with sketches and paintings of never consummated attractions. A video interview with Uncle Walt runs continuously.

The 1,000-room **Disneyland Hotel**, (1150 West Cerritos, Tel: 714-778 6600), is itself a small-scale resort with baby-sitter referrals, restaurants, a shopping center, video game room, themed swimming pools, sandy 'beach' and a (free) nightly performance by colored dancing fountains.

Bright and comfortable rooms begin at a fairly stiff $180, and be aware: room service charges are exorbitant. But you can buy your admission ticket at the hotel and monorail travel and early admission to the park are included, as they are at the new **Pacific Hotel** (Tel: 714-999 0990). It's obviously convenient to stay here, as part of the whole excursion to Disneyland, and take the monorail to the park, but if your budget doesn't run to that, there are dozens of alternatives.

Three of the avenues flanking Disneyland itself – **Katella**, **West Street** and **Harbor Boulevard** – are lined with motels whose billboards scream out highly competitive prices. Along Harbor Boulevard at some times in the year it's not hard to find rooms for under $50, single or double, with a cluster of places near the corner of Katella offering rooms for as little as $35. If you have a car and are on a budget, it pays to drive around and comparison-shop. Parking in the Disneyland lot costs $7, but many hotels offer complimentary shuttle service.

South Bay

A day at the beach, a ride in a gondola, and a visit to the San Juan Capistrano mission.

—To book a gondola around the Naples canals, call 562-433 9595—

Don't wait until March 19 when the swallows fly back to Capistrano to pay a visit to this 200-year-old mission; enjoy a day-long excursion by driving south through the various beach communities, around the Palos Verdes peninsula and through Long Beach on the way. (MTA225 buses from the LAX Transit Center cover most of this route, connecting with MTA232 into Long Beach.)

Drive south along the Pacific Coast Highway, turning right at **Manhattan Beach** Boulevard for a peek at that particular community. Next down the coast are **Hermosa Beach,** site of the National Volleyball championships, and **Redondo Beach.** All sites have piers. To see some magnificent homes, leave the PCH as it swerves inland at Ave H in Redondo Beach, heading south on Palos Verdes Drive and then hugging the coast on the Paseo del Mar.

Just past the Golden Shores shopping center is a lighthouse be-side which, at the **Point Vicente Interpretive Center** (daily, 10am–5pm), are telescopes to look for passing whales (December to spring), a small exhibit (admission fee) which includes an informative **whale-watching video,** plus earphones to listen to the mournful voices of these loveable monsters and a relief map of the peninsula showing how mountainous is the terrain. There are nice grassy grounds suitable for picnicking (bring your own food and drink) and leaflets identifying the various plants to be found on the **Botanic Trail**.

Point Vicente lighthouse

Beach still life

About a mile further on is the wood and glass **Wayfarers Chapel**, designed by Frank Lloyd Wright's son Lloyd, whose inspiration is said to have been Northern California's majestic redwood trees. It was built in 1951 as a memorial to the 18th-century Swedish theologian Emmanuel Swedenborg. Walking around the peaceful gardens to the sound of songbirds, a fountain and the gurgling stream is very tranquilizing. There are services in the chapel at 11am every Sunday.

Palos Verdes Drive segues into 25th Street from which we turn left on Gaffey (State Highway 110) and up to Highway 47 over the Vincent Thomas Bridge then straight ahead through **Long Beach** on Ocean Avenue. Out in the bay, take a close look at the **palm-fringed island** with the tall towers: it's actually one of four man-made islands created by a consortium of oil companies to hold (and conceal) all the working oil derricks which for 25 years have been tapping one of the richest offshore fields in the United States. The towers are lighted at night.

From Long Beach, you can take an MTA232, then a No 147 bus ride westwards along the coast to **San Pedro**, headquarters of Southern California's fishing fleet which once distinguished this town as a genuine fishing port. All the original construction is gone, of course, replaced by a pseudo 19th-century enterprise called **Ports O' Call Village** which surprisingly turns out to be imaginatively and attractively done. It consists of several blocks of New England 'weathered' shops – 75 in all plus 15 restaurants – in complementing and matching styles that are a joy to walk around. Harbor tours and fishing trips go from here (as well as the *Catalina Express*, detailed in the next tour).

There's oodles of free parking space beside which a heroic fisherman statue proclaims, 'Lo, the fisherman, for his harpoon, hook and net have long harvested the endless sea.' Across the harbor from the *Queen Mary* and opposite the Convention Center, Long Beach's newest attraction is the impessive **Aquarium of the Pacific** (Shoreline Drive, daily 10am–6pm, Tel: 562-951 1683).

From Olive Street in downtown LA, an MTA446 bus will take you directly into San Pedro where at 7th and Pacific transfer for MTA147 to go to Ports O' Call. From there you can walk over to Pier 53 and look around a preserved merchant ship from World War II, the *Lane Victory*.

At Belmont, a swing leftwards along Livingston Drive intersects with 2nd Street from which we now skirt the beach of **Alamos Bay**. Time for a stop at **Gondola Getaway** on East Ocean Beach Boulevard where we can take a unique, 1-hour tour in a real gondola

San Juan Capistrano

along canals which pass the elegant homes of neighboring **Naples**. Operating 11am–11pm daily, the gondolas carry from two to six people and are stocked with bread, cheese, salami, wineglasses and ice (but bring your own drinks).

Back to the Pacific Coast Highway which bypasses Seal Beach and runs beside the ecological wetlands preserve just before Bolsa Chica state beach. At **Huntington Beach**, slow down to allow the surfers to carry their boards across the road. Many of the communities around here are in dispute about which most deserves the title 'Surf City' but Huntington claims to have the best case.

Past Newport Bay at the intersection of Poppy Avenue in Corona del Mar, a red English phone booth stands outside the ivy-covered **Five Crowns**, an imitation English pub. Near **El Moro Beach**, an attractive cove before **Laguna Beach** (whose annual Pageant of the Masters in July and August presents tableaux of famous paintings with costumed participants; Tel: 714-494 1345 for dates), an occasional pelican can be seen.

We make a final stop on this southbound drive at **Dana Point Harbor** to browse through the shops, then it's off on Del Obispo Street to **Camino Capistrano** on which is located the famous **mission** (open daily 8.30am–5pm), seventh in the chain of 21 established by Franciscan padres late in the 18th century.

Naples gondola

Father Junipero Serra founded nine of the missions, this one included, and his statue stands beside the ruined **Great Stone Church** to our right as we enter. The **Serra Chapel** behind the church is the oldest still-in-use building in all of California. Pick up a free map which identifies where the swallows' nests can be found during their residence between their arrival on St Joseph's Day, March 19 and their departure for warmer climes on October 23. The swallows are almost always on time, but even if they're not, the event is marked here by a **week-long festival**.

The **lovely gardens** were added this century but the main courtyard itself was always the central focus of the mission, being the site of rodeos in the old days.

Visit a beautiful island only an hour from the mainland.

—Call 310-519 1212 or 800-464 4228 for a reservation on the Catalina Express—

With its steep and rugged canyons, 54 miles of coastline and pocket-sized capital of Avalon, this temperate island 22 miles off the coast charms even the most jaded traveler who has come to regard Southern California as the capital of automania. Here there are no rental cars and the environmentally-oriented local authority has guaranteed that almost two-thirds of the island will always remain in its natural state. The first steamship service to the island began in 1888 at a time when pigeons were still being used to carry messages to and from the mainland.

We begin early in the day by taking the *Catalina Express* from Long Beach, zipping across to **Avalon** in one hour. The 5-minute walk into town passes a couple of places which rent bicycles or the ubiquitous golf carts which are the main personal transportation (residents here wait 6 years before being allowed to own a car) but that's for another day. On this visit we will explore the island by taking a few tours. Stop at the **Visitors' Bureau** on the pier to book before doing anything else.

First comes the 45-minute inspection of the **Casino** at the far end of the harbor which achieved national fame more than half a cen-

Catalina harbor

Casino mural

tury ago with broadcasts of such famous big bands as Count Basie playing in the Art Deco ballroom to five thousand dancers at a time. Built in 1929 at a cost of $2 million, the Casino's theater with a full-size organ was the first in America to be built especially for the new talking movies.

Walking back into town, drop by the hillside complex called **Solomon's Landing** (across from the Via Casino archway). Here among the pricey restaurants is a souvenir shop where, while listening to Al Jolson records, you can admire products from the long-defunct Catalina Pottery and other memorabilia including sheet music of songs about the island: *Catalina Is Calling Me, When Roses Bloom in Avalon, Catalina Aloha-Oe*.

On the glass-bottomed boat trip which starts from the pier and take about 40 minutes, it's fascinating to peer into the shallow waters just outside the harbor to watch the multi-colored fish darting in and out of a seaweed 'garden.' The fronds of kelp, swaying to the motion of the boat, seem to be dancing to a hidden music with the little fish acting as random soloists.

To really appreciate Catalina, we devote most of the afternoon to the **Inland Motor Tour**, which takes almost 4 hours but heads right up through the mountains to the island's airport. In the process it makes a stop at **El Rancho Escondido**, the Wrigley-owned ranch where Arabian horses are reared. Sipping iced lemonade, watch from the stands as an immaculately trained horse is put through its paces to demonstrate its skill and intelligence. Then it's onwards along the old stagecoach route across the island, passing old Indian sites and admiring secluded bays.

Descendants of General Phineas Banning, who operated the earliest stagecoach routes across the West, once owned most of Catalina, and began the process of turning it into the tourist resort it eventually became. When William Wrigley, the chewing gum tycoon, acquired the island after the great fire of 1919, he built the 1,000-bed luxury Hotel St Catherine at **Descanso Beach** west of town, a magnificent mansion on Mt Ada (now owned by the University of Southern California) and started the Catalina Pottery to provide tiles for other projects. The Wrigley family still owns about 15 percent of the island, donating the remainder to the nonprofit Island Conservancy which takes its responsibilities seriously.

Although 'discovered' by the Portuguese navigator Don Juan Rodriguez Cabrillo in 1542 and claimed for Spain as a safe anchorage for its Europe-bound treasure galleons 60 years later,

Catalina had actually been inhabited by Indians for thousands of years. Two centuries after the Spaniards arrived, the Indians were pretty much eliminated by Russian hunters in their search for sea otter pelts. Later visitors, mostly American, included traders, pirates, smugglers and even miners who mistakenly believed the island to be rich in gold and other minerals.

Wild fauna such as the bald eagle, fox, goat, buffalo and wild boar, have been protected and their numbers expanded since the Island Conservancy took over. On the bus tour, we'll almost certainly see a couple of buffalo, descendants of a herd brought here when Zane Grey's *The Vanishing American* was filmed on the island in 1925. The house that Grey ('Avalon... is the most delightful and comfortable place I ever visited') once owned has since become the **Zane Grey Pueblo Hotel** (Tel: 310-510 0966).

A stop is made at the airport, at 1,600ft Catalina's highest point, where a small display includes historical pictures and a diorama featuring local animals. Apart from flights to San Diego, there is no longer a scheduled service from the airport. There is a bus connecting with Avalon four times daily (Tel: 310-510 0143 for schedule), an alternative way to get into the mountains from town.

There are other options: 1-hour tours to see flying fish or sealions; a 2-hour inspection of the **Skyline Drive**; and two evening tours, one of which includes dinner at **Two Harbors**, the island's other main community. Even downtown itself can be done in a group aboard the guided 40-minute tram tour, although Avalon is so small it's more fun to aimlessly wander, admiring the local tiles on the **Serpentine Wall** opposite the beach or on the fountain in Wrigley Plaza, shopping and eating.

Leave yourself some time for a stroll through the back streets where most of the tiny houses are built on lots that originally housed tents. Drop by Franklin Pyke's bookshop on **Metropole Street** and look at his old postcards.

It's a stiff climb up **Avalon Canyon** – almost 2 miles – to the 37-acre **Wrigley Memorial** and **Botanical Garden**, but once you make it, you can stroll among trees, plants and succulents, many of which are endemic to this island. There are, of course, also taxis if by now you're feeling tired.

Catalina cruising

Santa Barbara

Head north to discover a colonial town and great beaches.

The drive to Santa Barbara (up the Pacific Coast Highway and then US 101 after Oxnard) takes under 3 hours. It is a pleasant city, with its architecture almost entirely in idealized Spanish Colonial style; after a disastrous earthquake in 1925 the city's leaders imposed a mandatory building code that prohibited anything ugly or unharmonious.

For anyone who abhors driving, the city is readily accessible by a Greyhound bus which deposits passengers in the center of town, only 2 blocks from the handsome **Spanish-Moorish courthouse** at Anacapa and Figueroa streets. Take the elevator to the roof to admire the panoramic view of gently-sloping red-tile roofs and, immediately below, the multi-level lawn, very much in favor for lunchtime picnics. After returning to ground level, we're ready to begin our short scenic route of the downtown area. It's called, appropriately enough, the 'Red Tile Tour.'

Mission Santa Barbara

Walk straight past **the library** to State Street, passing (or stopping to visit) the **Museum of Art** on the way. Turn left along Carrillo to visit the **Hill-Carrillo Adobe**, built by Daniel Hill in 1826 for his Spanish bride. It was the city's first home with a wooden floor. Continue down Anacapa Street to Canon Perdido Street. The block to our left, bordered by the **Cañedo Adobe** (c 1782), is where Santa Barbara began, centered around the **Presidio** with its chapel and parade grounds, more restored adobes and the **Historical Society Museum** which contains costumes and many ancient documents (Tuesday–Saturday 10am–5pm; Sunday noon–5pm; free). Afterwards, head back towards State Street to admire the **Santiago de la Guerra Adobe** (1827), the original home of the Presidio's commander and his family. The plaza here is where the

Detail from courthouse

city council first met in 1850, an event still celebrated every August with a fiesta. Here also is the enticing cobbled area **El Paseo** (or 'the street in Spain' as tourist officials call it). It is by far the most attractive place in town to shop and sip a coffee at one of the outdoor cafés around the fountain. We end our 'official' tour here.

Anyone who wants to explore further should head back to **State Street**, and go south, where the road terminates at attractive **Stearns Wharf**, the oldest on the west coast. This pier offers everything – seafood stands, restaurants, wine tasting, a marine museum, fishing – and is the starting point for **whale-watching boat trips** which set off daily in spring to catch glimpses of the heavyweight mammals returning north with their offspring after a winter spent off the Baja coast.

Alternatively, you could first head north up State Street and turn right for 3 or 4 blocks to **Mission Santa Barbara** (daily 9am–5pm; admission fee; Tel: 805-682 4713) which with its twin bell towers is generally regarded as the most beautiful of the remaining missions. Founded in 1786, it was damaged in both of the area's major earthquakes (1812, 1925) but has been lovingly restored. It is still in use as a parish church. Don't miss the interesting museum which has many relics of the days when Chumash Indians lived at the mission while being 'trained' to undertake useful tasks by their Spanish overlords.

More about Indian life preceding the occupation can be studied 2 blocks to the north in the **Museum of Natural History** (daily 9am–5pm, admission fee) with its interesting array of inanimate animals, birds and fish. There's another attraction in this area al-

El Paseo Mall

though it's more than a mile to the north up Mission Canyon Road: the **Botanic Garden** (Tel: 805-682 4726).

This has walking trails through 60 acres of native flowers, shrubs and cacti. Flowing through the garden is water from Mission Creek, a dam built by Spanish friars with Indian labor two centuries ago. Following the **Tunnel Trail** up the Santa Ynez Mountains towards La Cumbre Peak (3,989ft) will bring you to a group of waterfalls and – somewhat higher – impressive views of the coastline.

Time now, if you haven't already done so, to head back down State Street to the pier. On the way you might want to make a short diversion to Chapala and Montecito streets to admire what's said to be the largest tree of its kind in America. It's a Moreton Bay **fig tree**, native to Australia and planted here in 1877, since which time its branches have grown to cover an area of 160ft. One long block further west along Montecito is a Victorian mansion still furnished in the style of the period, the **Fernald House**. Adjoining it is an adobe house built in 1854 from the timbers of a wrecked ship.

If you feel like swimming, the wonderful beaches of Santa Barbara are justly famous and stretch for a considerable distance along both sides of town. About 20 miles northwest of town, adjoining US 1, **El Capitan State Beach** has elicited raves from many visitors who have often found the wooded campsites with ocean views – there are 140 of them, each with its own barbecue grill – pleasantly uncrowded. There are hiking trails, plenty of rest rooms and a camp store (for reservations call 1-800-444 7275).

Beaches at the southern end of Santa Barbara end temporarily in a tree-shaded promontory dominated by the classy **Miramar Resort Hotel.** Not far away, beside State Highway 1, is the charming **Montecito Inn** which has been popular with refugees from Hollywood, 3 hours' drive away, since the 1920s when one of its original owners was Charlie Chaplin.

If you're driving back to Los Angeles, it's worth stopping at **Ventura**, not only to admire the tiny **Mission San Buenaventura**, built in 1782, but to plan a trip to the secluded **Channel Islands**, a national park whose meticulous management lays great emphasis on preservation. Most visitors are those on day-long tours operated by **Island Packers** (recorded information: 805-642 7688). Sightings of sea lions, seals, dolphins and exotic birds are frequent.

PALM SPRINGS

Head south and east for a trip into the desert.

Although Palm Springs is the main city in the desert area, it has come to refer also to several nearby communities, many of which have springs of their own (first judged to be therapeutic by the local Agua Caliente Indians). The area is best known for golf courses and swimming pools: there are about 80 of the former and approximately 7,000 of the latter. These and other attractions bring about 2 million visitors every year, lured by a warm, mostly dry climate but, be warned, in summer it can be exhaustingly humid). The San Bernadino freeway, then Interstate 10, will bring you to Palm Springs in just under 3 hours, not a very fascinating trip until you reach **Cabazon** where you'll want to pause at the truckstop called the **Wheel Inn** to look at the **giant concrete dinosaurs** towering 30ft above the highway.

From here onwards there are spectacular views of hillsides covered with row after row of **steel windmills** generating electric power the natural way. For $18 you can take a 45-minute tour in a golf cart. You can also detour en route to town along I-10 to **Cathedral City**, where a museum devoted to silent screen star Mary

California cruisin'

Fountains and mountains

Pickford is the centerpiece of the **Pickford Center**. Turning right onto State Highway 111 leads down **Palm Canyon Drive**, one of the two parallel main streets around which the town is structured. Merchants along the street enhance the already busy

street on Thursday and Friday nights (except in midsummer) with a sort of sidewalk party featuring street entertainers, music and refreshments.

Most of the things visitors want to see in Palm Springs itself are comfortably within walking distance, especially when the journey is broken at one of the pleasant sidewalk cafés, some of which continuously spray out a fine mist to cool the neighboring air. The **Desert Fashion Plaza** on this palm-lined thoroughfare is as upscale as it sounds, although it does stage occasional free concerts.

A block or two further down, we'll start by looking around what passes for an 'old town' area, the tiny **Village Green Heritage Center**. The center consists of the restored **McAllum Adobe**, which was the home of one of the region's pioneers, a couple of other century-old buildings – one built from old railroad ties – and a recreated **general store** from the 1930s with genuine canned and packaged goods bearing their old labels.

In this ultra-chic, ultra-modern town, this is more interesting than almost anything except the **Desert Museum** (closed Mondays), behind the Fashion Plaza, with its dioramas of the desert and old Indian artifacts. Walk (or drive) down to 1701 South Palm Canyon Drive to **Moorten's Botanical Garden**, for an insight into the local flora and fauna. Here in this living museum, thousands of trees, cacti and flowers line the nature trails. One block east of Palm Canyon Drive is **Indian Avenue**, the other main street. It is similar to the other thoroughfare, but interesting in itself for being the northern route into the desert, first to **Desert Hot Springs** and in about 1 hour's drive to Joshua Tree.

Joshua Tree National Monument is a vast parkland filled with strange rocks, fascinating flora and fauna and the tall, fibrous plants after which it is named. It's unlikely you'll see any of the mostly nocturnal animals other than lizards (kangaroo rats, coy-

Palm Springs pleasures

otes, rattlesnakes) unless you stay overnight in one of the camping grounds. From the highest points, the view is all the way across the Coachella Valley to the Salton Sea. The easiest and most interesting way to visit this area, the similarly unspoiled **Santa Rosa Mountains** and the **Indian Canyons** with their cool palm oases is via Desert Adventures (Tel: 619-324 3378), an ecologically-minded tour company with extraordinarily knowledgeable guides. Among other attractions, they can take you to inspect the infamous San Andreas Fault.

Even if you don't have time to explore the wilderness, be sure to visit **The Living Desert** (for information call: 619-346 5694), an extensive nature park 15 miles southeast of Palm Springs, filled with eagles, bighorn sheep, interesting and irresistible animals – don't overlook the loveable meerkats – and desert flowers and cacti. You'll see from the map you're handed at the entrance that it's a lengthy walk around the park, but fortunately there are shady areas and drinking fountains at frequent intervals. Last admission is at 4.30pm; it is closed mid-June through August.

Just north of town is the **Aerial Tramway** which during an awe-

some 14-minute ride through a canyon that once was the site of an Indian village, climbs to an 8,516ft peak of the **San Jacinto Mountains**. At the top from the deck of the restaurant (with its cocktail bar and gift shop) there's an understandably magnificent view of Palm Springs and the **Coachella Valley** in which it sits. (Take a jacket, especially if you want to explore some of the 54 miles of trails.) Overnight camping is allowed up here in the wilderness with permits available on site. In winter, equipment is rented for cross-country skiing (for information call: 619-325 4227).

A large number of visitors take

Desert flowers

the opportunity to indulge in some sporting activity while in this desert resort area. In Santa Barbara itself, the younger crowd flock to the **Oasis Water Resort Villa Hotel** (1500 Gene Autry Trail, Tel: 800-247 4664) whose hotel rooms surround a health club, enormous swimming pool, volley ball courts and seven breathtaking, daredevil water slides. At the south end of town, along Toledo Avenue, is **Smoke Tree Stables** (Tel: 619-327 1372), where horses can be rented for short or long rides into the canyons. A map of the numerous bicycle routes located around town is available from the **Visitor Information Office** at 2781 North Palm Canyon Drive, near Tramway Road.

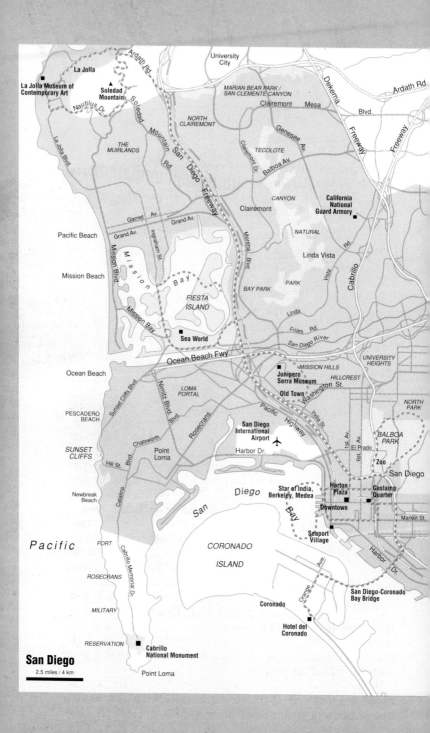

University
City

La Jolla

Ardath Rd.

Ardath Rd.

La Jolla Museum of
Contemporary Art

Soledad
Mountain

MARIAN BEAR PARK /
SAN CLEMENTE CANYON

Dekema
Freeway

Freeway

Blvd.

Clairemont   Mesa

Nautilus Dr.

Soledad

NORTH
CLAIREMONT

THE
MUIRLANDS

Mountain San Diego Freeway

Rd.

Genesee Av.

Clairemont Dr.

TECOLOTE

Balboa Av.

La Jolla Blvd

Garnet   Av.

Grand Av.

Pacific Beach

Grand Av.

Clairemont

CANYON

California
National
Guard Armory

Ingraham St.

Mission Blvd.

Mission Beach

B a y

Morena   Blvd.

NATURAL

Linda Vista

Cabrillo

Vista   Rd.

Mission

FIESTA
ISLAND

BAY PARK

PARK

UNIVERSITY
HEIGHTS

Mission Bay

Sea World

Linda

Friars   Rd.

San Diego River

Ocean Beach Fwy.

MISSION HILLS

Junipero
Serra Museum

HILLCREST

Ocean Beach

LOMA
PORTAL

Old Town

Washington St.

NORTH
PARK

PESCADERO
BEACH

Sunset Cliffs Blvd

Nimitz Blvd.

Rosecrans

Pacific

Highway

India St.

BALBOA
PARK

SUNSET
CLIFFS

Chatsworth

San Diego
International
Airport

El Prado

Zoo

1st. Av.

6th Av.

San Diego

Hill St.

Point
Loma

Harbor Dr.

Newbreak
Beach

Catalina

Diego

Star of India,
Berkeley, Medea

Horton
Plaza

Gaslamp
Quarter

Downtown

Market St.

Pacific

FORT

Cabrillo Memorial Dr.

San

Bay

CORONADO

ISLAND

Seaport
Village

Harbor   Dr.

ROSECRANS

Orange   Av.

San Diego-Coronado
Bay Bridge

MILITARY

Coronado

RESERVATION

Cabrillo
National Monument

Hotel del
Coronado

San Diego

2.5 miles / 4 km

Point Loma

San Diego

Take a leisurely route south towards the Mexican border.

It takes under 3 hours to drive to San Diego via freeways 5 and 805, but an Amtrak train from LA's Union Station will deposit you conveniently on the San Diego waterfront (or you can alight at **Del Mar**, a couple of stops before, and sit on the beach virtually in front of the station). Del Mar racetrack (July through September; Tel: 619-755 1141) owes its origins to such Hollywood founders as Desi Arnaz and Bing Crosby, who sought a playground outside Los Angeles.

San Diego harbor

If you're driving to San Diego, there are a number of diversions that can be taken along the way. How long you spend in each place, and in San Diego itself, depends on how long your trip can be extended. If there's time, be sure to make a diversion off the Pacific Coast Highway into **Torrey Pines** and park in a large unpaved lot from which you can watch daredevil hang-gliders soar off the 300ft cliffs. Below is **Blacks' Beach**, famous for its nude bathers.

Alternatively, you could turn off at **Santa Ana** and visit **Newport Beach** and **Balboa** en route. Newport's harbor is enclosed by the Balboa peninsula where Newport Boulevard becomes Balboa Boulevard. Stop at the intersection with Washington Street and have brunch at the Bon Appetite bakery. Then continue down to Main Street to admire the **Balboa Pavilion**, built in 1905 as a railroad terminal, with its distinctive but totally unnecessary steeple. If you get here early enough, you'll find fishing boats unloading their catch just behind the pavilion.

Similar in age is the ferry, which makes the bargain-price 3-minute trip from the end of Palm Street to **Balboa Island**. The island dazzles with million-dollar homes and classy shops and cafés.

On your way back you can see the former homes of John Wayne and Roy Rogers on nearby islands. From the **Balboa Pier** you can admire the kite-flyers, frisbee-throwers, body-surfers and sunbathers.

Other stops could be made on the outskirts of San Diego itself. **La Jolla** was for years America's wealthiest zipcode, with its grand houses, scenic headland location and chic 'village' shops and restaurants.

Further south comes **Mission Bay**, once a swamp but now an immense aquatic playground with fishing, boat rentals, resort hotels and campgrounds. The San Diego Symphony presents its summer

San Diego zoo

pop concerts on the shore; nearby is **Sea World** (daily 10am–5pm, until 11pm in summer), a 135-acre oceanarium with a performing cast of sea lions, walruses, dolphins and penguins, headed by Shamu, a 2-ton whale.

North of the airport, the **Old Town** area is where the city first began. On top of the hill where the presidio once stood is the **Junipero Serra Museum** (Tel: 619-297 3258) commemorating the padre who built the first of his missions near here in 1769. The mission-style museum, erected in 1929, stores the city's early history. The 6-block area below, where the community's first citizens lived, includes the **old plaza**, **museums**, **adobes**, restored Victorian homes and numerous colorful restaurants which are busiest at nighttime.

Buses run to Old Town from downtown San Diego.

The **San Diego Zoo** (daily 9am–dusk) may be the best place to start your visit. Said to be the oldest zoo in America, it's located at the north end of **Balboa Park**. Admission includes a ride on Skyfari, which is an aerial tramway from which you can admire all the uncaged animals in their canyon habitats. Afterwards, walk through the park with its half-dozen museums (on Saturdays there are often free samples of food on offer) before going downtown. The same bus from the zoo also goes to **Seaport Village** with its theme cafés and century-old carousel.

A red trolley car runs all around downtown (and 12 miles south to the Mexican border), but everything is within fairly easy walking distance, including the full-rigged sailing ship *Star of India* (1863), the luxury steam yacht *Medea* (1904) and the former ferry boat *Berkeley* (which rescued survivors from the 1906 earthquake). These ships comprise part of the waterfront **Maritime Museum** (Tel: 619-234 9153) just north of the Amtrak station.

Adjoining the waterfront 'village' is the spiffy-looking downtown convention center opposite **Gaslamp Quarter**, a several block area of refurbished Victorian buildings now occupied by artists, galleries, trendy boutiques and cafés. A very good place to eat lunch is next door at **Horton Plaza**, a multi-level collection of stores, eating places (including a 1950s-style diner) and cinemas. The plaza's stylish design, layout and street performers combine to produce one of the most interesting malls in the West.

One other place must be seen: the **Hotel del Coronado** across San Diego Bay on **Coronado island**, which is reached via a toll bridge. The hotel 'co-starred' with Tony Curtis and Marilyn Monroe in the movie *Some Like It Hot* and is unquestionably the area's most popular attraction. It is a superlative example of elegant Victorian architecture (1888), complete with all its geegaws and eccentricities. A dozen presidents have stayed here in the years since Thomas Edison personally installed the electric lighting.

Britain's then-Prince of Wales met his future wife here, the notorious Mrs Simpson, who lived on the grounds in a bungalow (which is still standing). Charles Lindbergh dropped by before and after his first trans-Atlantic flight, and author L Frank Baum is said to have used it as an inspiration for *The Wizard of Oz*. All these occasions are memorialized in a corridor lined with giant photographs. A ferry leaves the dock at Harbor Drive and Broadway in San Diego on the hour, 9am–10pm; it leaves the Coronado Old Ferry Landing at B Avenue and 1st Street every half-hour.

Nightime near Mexico

Los Angeles

Beverly Hills' glitzy **Rodeo Drive**, with such world-class establishments as Chanel, Armani and Neiman Marcus is still the epitome of conspicuous consumption, something of a tourist trap for those who know the price of everything but the value of nothing.

Two complexes here draw the biggest crowds: the **Rodeo Collection**, a pinkish mall on two levels specializing mostly in fashion (Nina Ricci, Sonia Rykiel) and the faux-cobbled winding street, **Two Rodeo Drive** (Tiffany, Cartier, Dior), built above a parking garage with free valet parking to resemble Rome's fashionable Via Condoti. Both **Giorgio Armani** and **Giorgio** (jewelry, perfume) have stores on Rodeo Drive.

A mile to the east is **Century City**, where the shopping center and marketplace boasts 140 stores, theaters, and restaurants whose validation will give you three hours of free parking. The Broadway, Los Angeles' century-old department store chain, operates a branch here as it does at the multi-level **Beverly Center** at La Cienega Boulevard and 3rd Street. Neon escalators ascend five floors past 200 stores large and small, plus a 13-screen movie theater and multi-level garage (don't forget where you parked your car).

Macy's department store is in the Beverly Center, with another branch downtown (750 West 7th). This is where you'll find a branch of the May Company which adjoins a gourmet food pavilion. Both I Magnin and Saks Fifth Avenue maintain branches on the 9600 block of Wilshire in **Beverly Hills**. The smaller mall of fashionable shops at **Sunset Plaza**, behind the sidewalk cafés on the 8000 to 9000 blocks of Sunset Boulevard, is also a pleasant shopping destination.

Two big department stores – Robinsons and The Broadway – anchor the highly attractive **Santa Monica Mall** at the foot of 3rd Street in the area of the same name. The pedestrian-only street is lined with sidewalk cafés and the enclosed area, with a department store at each end, features a score of different food counters with eating at central tables. Santa Monica has two other attractive shopping areas: **Montana Avenue**, north of Wilshire Boulevard, and **Main Street**, near the beach. Both places are dotted with attractive cafés and restaurants.

Smaller malls in **Glendale** and on the Valley side of **Topanga Canyon** Boulevard are among dozens of similar ones around town and in neighboring communities. Several interesting little shops are dotted among the eating places at the **Farmers Market** (Fairfax Avenue and 3rd Street). It's also worth checking out the little-known fashion district on East 9th Street downtown.

Also **downtown** is a subterranean shopping center with 55 shops under **Arco Plaza** on Flower & 5th streets, and the multi-level **Bonaventure Shopping Gallery** in the hotel of that name on Figueroa Street. For specialty shopping, try the Mexican style of **Olvera Street** and the **Japanese Village Plaza**, 327 East 2nd Street. LA's oldest bookstore, Fowler

This way for classy fashion

Fishing for a bargain

Brothers, 717 West 7th Street, started life as a church supply house in 1888 and has prospered ever since.

Melrose Avenue, with its whackily named stores, has lot some of its lustre with the famous Soap Plant having relocated to the trendy new **Los Feliz** area (around Hollywood Boulevard and Vermont). Some action has shifted around the corner onto **La Brea Avenue**, where the block-long **American Rag** (150 South La Brea) offers lots of clothing bargains.

Two invaluable and well-stocked **bookstores** are the Traveler's Bookcase (8375 West 3rd Street) and its next door neighbor the Cook's Library.

For **antiques**, Pasadena Antique Center, 480 South Fair Oaks Avenue, and Showcase Antiques (818-577 9660) in the same block, are good sources. Note also the Santa Monica Antiques Market, located at 1607 Lincoln Boulevard.

Pasadena's South Lake Avenue exudes a village-like ambience with top retailers spread over multi-level malls.

In search of **exotic food**? You might want to consider browsing around the five blocks of Hollywood Boulevard between Harvard and Kingsley. Beginning with the Bucharest Grocery and Deli with its emphasis on Near Eastern and Balkan foods at 5235 Hollywood Boulevard, you'll find a mouth-watering array of Thai, Iranian, Japanese and Russian restaurants, an Egyptian coffee house, an Armenian butcher, a Lebanese pastry shop, a Salvadoran tropical fruit store and a German delicatessen. Not to mention a Guatemalan market.

On I-5, south of Anaheim, is Costa Mesa whose massive **South Coast Plaza** truly offers one-stop shopping. There are more than 300 stores, including every major Southern California department store, an airline magazine once reported, "as well as the best and worst of the Beverly Hill boutiques."

Santa Barbara

The downtown **El Paseo Mall** on State Street near De La Guerra has been refurbished and is host to gift and clothing stores as well as galleries and restaurants. Other attractive, Spanish-style malls are **La Arcada Court**, with its pleasant courtyard, at State and Victoria streets, and **Paseo Nuevo,** anchored by Nordstrom and The Broadway department stores at State and Chapala. The city's biggest shopping mall, **La Cumbre Plaza**, at 3800 State Street, houses 60 stores including Sears, Robinson's and a Disney store, opposite which the café run by my old friend Jim Buckley is reputed to have the best coffee in town. For antiques, stroll along **Brinkerhoff Avenue**, named after the city's first doctor, where not only his house but other Victorian homes have been restored.

Palm Springs

The desert town is renowned for its chic shopping opportunities centered around a trio of malls on Palm Canyon Drive: **The Canyon Collection** in a rustic courtyard, the classy **Desert Fashion Plaza** and the **Amado Center**.

San Diego

This is a shopper's delight, with **Mission Valley** the premier area; its two neighboring malls house some 175 shops and restaurants. Many interesting stores can be found in the **Old Town** area too. **Downtown** is home, not only to the fanciful **Horton Plaza** with its imaginative architecture, theaters and restaurants, but also to numerous boutiques along the **Embarcadero** and craft shops in the restored **Gaslamp Quarter**. And only a trolley ride away is the bargain-lovers' Mexican city of **Tijuana**.

Eating Out

Trendy foodies in Los Angeles, where you'll probably spend much of your time, can hardly wait for the *Los Angeles Magazine* or the Sunday restaurant pages of the *Los Angeles Times* to tell them the latest grazing place. Going out to eat here has always been a social experience. LA, after all, was where the concept of 'restaurants-as-theater' got its start. Visitors usually like to go to places where stars might be spotted, but oddly enough this isn't always the same thing as a society restaurant.

Any place initiated by celebrity chefs Wolfgang Puck or Joachim Splichal is usually a safe bet, though. A *LA Times'* listing titled 'Seeing Stars' included such familiar 'power' spots as Spago, Morton's, The Olive, Le Dome, Nate 'n' Al's Delicatessen and – surprisingly – Pink's, the elegant hotdog stand on La Brea where you'll sometimes find celebs wolfing a wiener at midnight.

Prices listed include a meal for two, without wine: $ = under $25; $$ = $25–35; $$$ = $35 and above.

Los Angeles

Beverly Hills

ED DEBEVIC'S
134 N. La Cienega
Tel: 310-659 1952
Comfort food, sassy waitpersons, wild signs, crazy scenes and general mayhem. $

IL PASTAIO
400 N. Canon Drive
Tel: 310-205 5444
An outpost of Santa Monica's Celestino Drago, with the brother working in the kitchen. $$

NATE 'N' AL
414 N. Beverly Drive
Tel: 310-274 0101
Veteran, no frills Jewish deli acclaimed as best in the West. $$

PIAZZA RODEO
208 N. Rodeo Drive
Tel: 310-275 2428
Strategically situated outdoor terrace in chic shopping terrain. $$

GINZA SUSHI-KO
218 Via Rodeo
Tel: 310-247 8839
Maybe the most expensive restaurant in LA. No menu, but fish is flown in from Tokyo daily. $$$

SPAGO
176 N. Carlton Drive
Tel: 310-385 0880
Wolfgang Puck's base with leafy trees and always interesting recipes. $$$

THE GRILL
9560 Dayton
Tel: 310-276 0615
Expensive power lunch hangout which is discreetly hidden away just north of Wilshire. Outstanding crabcakes served here. $$$

JACKSON'S FARM
439 N. Beverly Drive
Tel: 310-273 5578
Deli-style indoors, sidewalk tables and

expensive sandwiches made with crusty baguettes. $$$

CRUSTACEAN
9646 Santa Monica Boulevard
Tel: 310-205 8990
Roasted Dungeness crab is the speciality in this Asian spot whose decor includes a fish-filled stream. $$$

MR CHOW
344 N. Camden Drive
Tel: 310-278 9911
Long famous celebrity favorite 'where stars actually show up to get away from being seen,' says *Los Angeles* magazine. $$$

Downtown and Environs

PHILIPPE THE ORIGINAL
1001 N. Alameda
Tel: 213-628 3781
Has been serving the French dip sandwich for 90 years. Hey, why do you think it's called 'the original'? $

ENGINE CO. NO. 28
644 S. Figueroa
Tel: 213-624 6996
Former firehouse that retains some brass and leather fittings and serves comfort food. $$

OCEAN SEAFOOD
750 N. Hill Street
Tel: 213-687 3088
The best seafood in Chinatown and the best dim sum lunch in LA. $$

A THOUSAND CRANES
New Otani Hotel
120 S. Los Angeles Street
Tel: 213-253 9255
Refined Japanese cuisine overlooking the rooftop garden. Sunday brunch is best. $$$

AZALEA RESTAURANT & BAR
New Otani Hotel
120 S. Los Angeles Street
Tel: 213-253 9235
Wood, brass and marble surroundings in a dining room with 24-ft ceiling. American cuisine with Japanese touches. $$$

CICADA
617 S. Olive Street
Tel: 213-655 5559
Owned by Stephanie, wife of composer Bernie Taupin, it's popular with Music Center habitués for pre-concert dinners. Specializes in Northern Italian cuisine. $$$

CAFE PINOT
700 W. 5th Street
Tel: 213-239 6500
'Eccentrically delicious' food says a local critic. Great setting in garden adjoining library. $$$

McCORMICK & SCHMICK'S
633 W. 5th Street
Tel: 213-629 1929
The biggest seafood restaurant in LA; there's also a branch on Rodeo Drive. $$$

Pretty as a pizza

PACIFIC DINING CAR
1310 W. 6th Street
Tel: 213-483 6000
The city's oldest steakhouse is prime in both price and quality. $$$

At or Near the Coast

HAVANA MANIA
3615 Inglewood Avenue,
Redondo Beach
Tel: 310-725 9075
Beans and rice go well with the pork tenderloin with Cuban seasoning. $

VAN GOGH'S EAR
796 Main Street, Venice
Tel: 310-396 1987

Simple food, an amusing mural and customers arriving all night long. $

NEPTUNE'S NET
42505 Pacific Coast Highway, Malibu
Tel: 310-457 3095
Always crowded, never expensive, with tanks of seafood from which you can make your selection and specify how you want it cooked. $

TERRACE CAFE
Hotel Laguna, 425 S. Coast Highway, Laguna Beach
Tel: 949-494 1151
Pizza and other simple dishes served on a flowery patio overlooking the beach. $

CHEZ JAY
1657 Ocean Avenue, Santa Monica
Tel: 310-395 1741
Gloomy bar with a funky obscurity that's been enticing Hollywoodites for decades. Famous for Chez Jay banana mashed potatoes. $

TILLY'S TERRACE
304 Santa Monica Place
Tel: 310-393 1404
Rooftop terrace dining above Frank Gehry's famous mall. Mainly Mexican. $

FRITTO MISTO
601 Colorado Avenue, Santa Monica
Tel: 310-458 2829
The name means mixed fried vegetables, a dish well worth sampling here. $

MALIBU INN & RESTAURANT
22969 Pacific Coast Highway
Tel: 310-456 6106
Knick-knack filled roadside place with pictures of local celebs – and sometimes patronized by the stars themselves. $

Sun 'n' surf 'n' submarine sandwiches

JOE'S RESTAURANT
1023 Abbot Kinney Boulevard, Venice
Tel: 310-399 5811
Simple, consistently good fish dishes with a decade of faithful customers. $$

THE GATE OF INDIA
115 Santa Monica Boulevard
Tel: 310 656 1664
Vegetarian, tandoori and mixed grill dinners along with 19 different curries and traditional appetizers and desserts. $$

TOPPERS
111 2nd Street, Santa Monica
Tel: 310-393 8080
Continental/Mexican cuisine atop the Radisson Hotel. Coastline views and nightly guitar music. $$

JAMES' BEACH
60 N. Venice Boulevard, Venice
Tel: 310-823 5396
Locals clamor for the chili cheese fries and exotic fruity margaritas. $$

BORDER GRILL
1445 4th Street, Santa Monica
Tel: 310-451 1655
Spacious cantina with some delicious specialties, but oh! the noise. $$

JiRAFFE
502 Santa Monica Boulevard
Tel: 310-917 6671
Elegant, well-flavored 'rustic American/French cuisine'. Try the roast rabbit appetizer. $$

LAVANDE
Loews Santa Monica Beach Hotel
Tel: 310-576 3181
Provençal chef brilliantly cooks up his native fare. Try the roast squab with lavender. $$$

VINCENTI
11930 San Vicente Boulevard
Tel: 310-207 0127
Classically memorable spit-roasted fare from a world class chef. $$$

CAFE DEL REY
4451 Admiralty Way,

Marina Del Rey
Tel: 310-823 6395
Panoramic windows overlook the marina in this popular place. Don't miss the curried lobster chowder. *$$$*

THE PALM
9001 Santa Monica Boulevard
Tel: 310-550 8811
Movers and shakers hang out here. Fabulous lobsters, but if you can afford one (says *Los Angeles* magazine) 'your last movie did OK'. *$$$*

CANYON BISTRO
108 W. Channel Road, Santa Monica
Tel: 310-230 9110
Friendly but upscale neighborhood café with French cuisine. Try the *crêpes suzette*. *$$$*

Mexican meal

21 OCEAN FRONT
2106 W. Ocean Front,
Newport Beach
Tel: 714-675 2566
Expensive pan-fried abalone, good steaks and a view of Catalina. *$$$*

L'ARANCINO
8908 Beverly Boulevard
Tel: 310-858 5777
The best of Celestino Drago's many restaurants, specializing in Sicilian pasta with lots of herbs. *$$$*

ENCOUNTER
209 World Way, at the airport
Tel: 310-215 5151
Atop the unique theme building at LAX is this dining and dancing spot, designed appropriately by Walt Disney Imagineering. *$$$*

PRIME TIME STEAKS
4211 Admiralty Way
Tel: 310-82-STEAK
Aged beef along with chicken, lamb, lobster and a great view of the marina. *$$$*

Westside

THE GUMBO POT
Fairfax Avenue & West 3rd Street
Tel: 323-933 0358
Cajun fare in the best known of at least a dozen eateries offering *al fresco* lunch in the Farmers' Market. *$*

SWING CAFE
8545 Santa Monica Boulevard
Tel: 310-652 8838
Informal hangout offering everything from turkey chile to English cottage pie and vegetarian fare. *$*

TASTE OF ASIA
8871 Santa Monica Boulevard
Tel: 310-289 1106
Oriental fast food in a casual setting. *$*

THE APPLE PAN
1081 W. Pico Boulevard
Tel: 310-475 3585
Seems to have been here forever serving hamburgers, but what hamburgers! Lunch only. *$*

CAFE 50S
11623 Santa Monica Boulevard
Tel: 310-479 1955
'Where you eat to the beat'. *$*

BARNEY'S BEANERY
8447 Santa Monica Boulevard
tel: 323-654 2287
Pool tables, funky clientele, 280 brands of beer and great ambience. *$*

TAIL O' THE PUP
329 N. San Vicente Boulevard
Tel: 310-652 4517
Landmark hotdog stand now 40 years in business. *$*

FABULOUS CAFE
6270 Sunset
Tel: 213-467 2882

Simple, inexpensive Italian cuisine, popular with Paramount employees from the nearby studios. $

WOK DELI
8579 Santa Monica Boulevard
Tel: 310-659 2311
Fast Chinese food that's better than your average fare. $

FLYING LEAP CAFE
2538 Hyperion Avenue
Tel: 213-661 0619
Charming, comfortable Silver Lake neighborhood place amusingly decorated and with friendly staff, serving typical American café food. $

LOLA'S
945 N. Fairfax Avenue
Tel: 213-736 5652
A handful of young stars found this place and most of them go for the sea scallops wrapped in smoky bacon and cooked in cognac. $$

YUJEAN KANG'S
8826 Melrose Avenue
Tel: 310-288 0806
Tea-smoked duck and other innovative Chinese dishes from a chef who earned his reputation at a similar place in Pasadena. $$

LIMBO
8338 W. 3rd Street
Tel: 213-866 8258
Spicy Caribbean food and, on weekends, live entertainment. $$

BOMBAY CAFE
12113 Santa Monica Boulevard
Tel: 310-820 2070
Southern Indian fare with all the traditional dishes and a few delectable surprises. $$

MUMBO CAFE
10032 Venice Boulevard, Culver City
Tel: 310-558 3106
Cuban and Caribbean with jerk chicken and seafood paella. $$

CAMPANILE
624 La Brea Avenue
Tel: 323-928 1447
Set in a graceful 1920s building with Moorish arches and bell tower. The food is Californian/Mediterranean, the fresh baked bread outstanding. $$$

SUR RESTAURANT AND GRILL
606 N. Robertson Boulevard
Tel: 310-289 2824
An Argentine bistro that has been justly praised for its grilled and barbequed meats. $$$

Pasadena

EL TAQUITO MEXICANO #2
467 N. Fair Oaks Avenue
Tel: 626-577 3918
Authentic Mexican home-cooking in unpretentious surroundings. Chips and salsa as good as it gets. $

THE RACK SHACK
58 E. Colorado Boulevard
Tel: 626-405 1994
Spicy aged meats are barbequed to perfection, accompanied by cornbread and salad. $

XIOMARA
69 N. Raymond Avenue
Tel: 626-796 2520
Latino-style food including *arepas, tamales* and Peruvian cheese sauces. $$

TWIN PALMS
101 W. Green Street
Tel: 818-57-PALMS
Delicious French cuisine under a vast tent, accompanied most nights by music or cabaret. $$$

ARROYO CHOP HOUSE
636 Arroyo Parkway
Tel: 626-577 7463
The style is the 1950s as are the jukebox selections; the steaks are fine. $$$

San Fernando Valley

PINOT BISTRO
12825 Ventura Boulevard, Studio City
Tel: 818-990 0500

Another outpost of renowned chef Joachim Splichal's French cuisine. *$$*

BARSAC BRASSERIE
4214 Lankershim Boulevard
Tel: 818-760 7081
Open kitchen serves Continental cuisine to a lively crowd from nearby Universal Studios. *$$*

CHA CHA CHA ENCINO
17499 Ventura Boulevard
Tel: 818-789 3600
Spicy food and lively music from the Caribbean islands. *$$*

FRANKIE'S
5538 Reseda Boulevard, Tarzana
Tel: 818-705 1295
Italian and Cajun-style cuisine with shrimp, chicken or crabcakes specials. *$$*

LA PERGOLA
15005 Ventura Boulevard,
Sherman Oaks
Tel: 818-905 8402
Pastas and lots of Italian-style vegetable dishes, with some ingredients grown out back. *$$$*

Outside Los Angeles

Santa Barbara

WOODY'S BODACEOUS BARBEQUE
5112 Hollister Avenue
Goleta
Tel: 805-967 3775
Menu is peppered with such words as 'chili', 'smoked', 'Cajun', 'grilled' and 'hot'. Takeout too. *$*

BLUE SHARK BISTRO
21 W. Victoria
Tel: 805-564 7100
Pastas, salads, seafood and chicken dishes predominate in this bright, tiny hideaway. *$$*

ANDRIA'S HARBORSIDE
336 W. Cabrillo Boulevard
Tel: 805-966 3000
Oyster bar, rack of lamb, Cajun blackened sirloin, jazz accompaniment. *$$*

CHINA PAVILION
1070 Coast Village Road
Tel: 805-565 9380
Vegetarian Buddha's Delight is a specialty dish, but plenty of duck, meat and fish as well. *$$*

LOUE'S
Upham Hotel,
1404 De La Vina
Tel: 805-963 7003
Elegant dining in century-old surroundings *$$$*

San Diego

THE BREAD BASKET RESTAURANT
Alpine Creek Shopping Center
Tel: 619-445 0706
The bakery produces 16 varieties of bread and breakfast is any time of the day you like. *$*

BAJA BREWING COMPANY
203 Fifth Avenue
Tel: 619-231 9279
'First Mexican brewpub in the US.' In the historic district downtown. *$*

FAST TRACK DIM SUM
4609 Convoy Street
Tel: 619-268 0888
Trendy Chinese kitchen whose customers keep coming back for more. *$$*

ATHENS MARKET TAVERN
109 West Street
Tel: 619-234 1955
'Food for the Gods' says *Gourmet* magazine. *$$$*

FISH WITH A VIEW
750 N. Harbor Drive
Tel: 619-234 4867
Fresh fish is flown in from New Zealand and the Gulf Coast. The interesting view is yacht-filled. *$$$*

BEST BUZZ
505 Laurel
Tel: 619-239 2222
'Refined, exciting and packed with knowledgeable customers' reports *Travel & Leisure*. *$$$*

Nightlife

There is an enormous range of nightlife in the Los Angeles area, most of it listed in the two free weekly papers *LA Weekly* and *New Times*. Hollywood and Santa Monica are the best areas but there is also much to be found in coastal areas to the south, **Pasadena's Old Town** area with its jazz clubs, bars and outdoor cafés, and the San Fernando Valley where **Universal City Walk** (free, but $5 for parking) offers jazz, restaurants, a magic club and lots of neon-lit street life.

Sunset Strip

The legendary haunt of all those '60s rockers is still a big draw. Within two or three blocks can be found the **Key Club** (Wednesday–Sunday, Tel: 310-274 5800) at 9039 Sunset Boulevard; **The Roxy** (every night, Tel: 310-276 2222) at #9009; **Whisky A Go-Go** (nightly, Tel: 310-652 4202) at #8901; and **Johnny Depp's Viper Room** (nightly, Tel: 310-358 1880) at #8852. All have live entertainment and dancing.

Further east are **The Comedy Store**, 8433 Sunset, Tel: 323-656 6225, whose

alumni include Roseanne Barr and Robin Willliams; **The Laugh Factory**, 8001 Sunset, Tel: 323-656 1336; the distinctive **House of Blues**, #8430, Tel: 323-848 5100, with music every night; and **The Body Shop**, 8250 Sunset, Tel: 323-656 1401, which has been presenting nightly strip shows for half a century.

West Hollywood

West Hollywwod is rife with nightlife ranging from dance clubs to cute little bars. **Des Villes**, 696 N. Robertson Boulevard, Tel: 310-289 1353, is somewhat untypical with its twin outdoor patios, comfortable lounge and top-notch sound system.

Clustered on or around the 8000 blocks of Santa Monica Boulevard is a predominantly gay area. In most places here gays are in the majority, such as at **Micky's**, 8857 Santa Monica Boulevard, Tel: 310 657 1176); **Rage**, 8911 Santa Monica Boulevard, Tel: 310-652 7055; and **Revolver**, 8851 Santa Monica Boulevard, Tel: 310-659 8851, all of which offer dancing and hip deejays. **The Palms**, 8572 Santa Monica Boulevard, Tel: 310-652 6188, is the oldest local lesbian bar and offers billiards, live entertainment and dancing. There's also dancing and live entertainment at **Love Lounge**, 657 N. Robertson Boulevard, Tel: 310-659 0471, and at **The Tempest Bar and Restaurant**, 7323 Santa Monica Boulevard, Tel: 310850 5115, a supper club whose over-the-top decor includes stained glass, crystal chandeliers and booths covered in burgundy brocade imprinted with cherubs.

The lights of LA

Santa Barbara nightspot

The pubs in West Hollywood tend to have pinball and pool tables while some add darts and video screens. **J. Sloan's**, 8623 Melrose Avenue, 310-659 0250, has the lot as well as dancing, karaoke and microbeers on tap. Other bars worth checking out include **Rafters**, 7994 Santa Monica Boulevard, Tel: 310-654 0396; **Numbers**, 8741 Santa Monica Boulevard, Tel: 310-652 7700; and **Hunter's**, 7509 Santa Monica Boulevard, Tel: 310-850 9428. **Guy's**, 8713 Beverly Boulevard, Tel: 310-360 0290, attracts the cigar aficionados; **Gold Coast**, 8228 Santa Monica Boulevard, Tel: 310-656 4879, is a low-key neighborhood bar; and **The Normandie Room**, 8737 Santa Monica Boulevard, Tel: 310-659 6204, is intimate, quiet and friendly.

Dance Spots

Other dance spots around town include the venerable **Art Deco Palace**, 1735 N. Vine, Tel: 213-462 3000, which books top rock groups; **The Conga Room** (5364 Wilshire, Tel: 213-938 1696, which specializes in Latin stars and the salsa beat; **Club 7969 Peanuts** at that number on Santa Monica Boulevard, Tel: 323-654 0280; **The Tempest**, 7323 Santa Monica Boulevard, Tel: 323-850 5115 (see *West Hollywood*); **Des Villes**, 696 N. Robertson, Tel: 310-289 1353 (see *West Hollywood*); **Luna Park** a few doors away, Tel: 310-652 0611; and the **Love Lounge** across the street, Tel: 310-659 0471.

Nightclubs and Cabaret

Television tycoon Merv Griffin spent a fortune to bring back the glamorous old **Coconut Club** (Tel: 310-285 1358), installing it in his glossy Beverly Hilton hotel at 9876 Wilshire. Friday and Saturday nights there's dancing to big bands, just like the old days. **Cinegrill** (Tel: 213-466 7000) in the Hollywood Roosevelt Hotel, has a long history of nightly entertainment, as does the **Atlas Supper Club** at 3760 Wilshire, adjoining the Wiltern Theater (Tel: 213-380 8400).

The Gardenia, 7066 Santa Monica Boulevard, Tel: 213-467 7444, specializes in sophisticated vocalists, Monday–Satur-

day, and **The Dresden Room**,1760 N. Vermont, Tel: 213-665 4294, has for a long time staged a nightly piano-bar lounge act. Here in Los Feliz a lively nighttime scene is developing. While there consider dining at the eclectic restaurant **Fred 62** 1850 N. Vermont Avenue, Tel: 213-667 0062; the **Drawing Room** and **Ye Rustic Inn** on nearby Hillhurst Avenue; also the trendy, little **Akbar** at 4356 Sunset.

Gay Nightlife

Axis, 652 N. La Peer Drive in Beverly Hills, Tel: 310-659 0471; **Micky's**, 8857 Santa Monica Boulevard, Tel: 310-657 1176); plus **Revolver**, Tel: 310-659 8851, and **Rage**, Tel: 310-652 7055, in the same block, are predominantly but not exclusively gay or lesbian dance venues. See also *Country and Western* listings.

Jazz and Blues

Catalina Bar & Grill, 3787 Cahuenga Boulevard, Tel: 213-466 2210, an intimate supper club that's always crowded, is the best spot to hear big name musicians. Reservations are a must. Afro-Cuban jazz is a feature of the dance joint **Cava**, 8384 West 3rd Street, Tel: 213-658 8898 (Thursday–Saturday). Jazz stars also appear at **Lunaria**, 10351 Santa Monica Boulevard, Tel: 310-282 8870; **Baked Potato**, 3787 Cahuenga Boulevard, Tel: 818-980 1615; and the **Jazz Bakery**, 3233 Helms Avenue, Tel: 310- 271 9039.

For blues, try **Harvelle's**, 1432 Fourth Street, Santa Monica, Tel: 310-395 1676. And over in the Valley don't overlook **Smokin' Johnnie's**, 11720 Ventura Boulevard, Studio City, Tel: 818-760 6631; **Cozy's Bar & Grill**, 14058 Ventura Boule-

vard, Tel: 818-986 6000; and **B.B. King's Blue Club** on the Universal CityWalk, Tel: 818-6BB-KING.

Leimert Park, southwest of downtown, has become the center of African-American artistic life with art galleries, restaurants, jazz clubs and shops. Between Leimert and Martin Luther King boulevards look for **5th Street Dick's Coffee House**, 3347 W. 43rd Street, Tel: 323-296 3970; **Bumpy's LA**; and the **Vision Complex Theater**, 4311 Degnan Boulevard, Tel: 323-295 9685.

Country and Western

Country and Western dancing takes place Friday and Saturday at **The Culver Saloon**, 11513 Washington Boulevard, Culver City, Tel: 310-391 1519, and nightly in the Valley at the **Cowboy Palace**, 21633 Devonshire in Chatsworth, Tel: 818-341 0166, a funny bar that terms itself 'the last real honky tonk'. Two other Country and Western clubs are in Burbank: **Crazy Jack's**, 4311 W. Magnolia Boulevard, Tel: 818-845 1121; and **Viva Fresh**, 900 Riverside Drive, Tel: 818-845 2425, a huge Mexican restaurant adjoining the equestrian center.

Folk and Rock

Doug Weston's Troubador, 9081 Santa Monica, Tel: 310-276 6168, has been showcasing folk and rock stars since the 1960s, as has the tiny **McCabe's Guitar Shop**, 3101 Pico Boulevard, Tel: 310- 828 4403. Singers are always in style at **Largo**, 432 N. Fairfax Avenue, Tel: 323- 852 1073.

Comedy Clubs

Bud Friedman's **The Improvisation**, 8162 Melrose, Tel: 323-651 2583, the oldest of the comedy clubs, is where many of today's best young comics got their start.

There's now a branch of The Improvisation at 6468 Santa Monica Boulevard, Tel: 213-694 2935.

Groundlings Theater, 7307 Melrose, Tel: 323-934 9700, was nominated by *LA Weekly* as 'the best improv team in town' and has spawned a number of stars over the years; **Acme Comedy Theater**, 135 N. La Brea, Tel: 323-525 0202, stages shows Friday–Sunday; free performances can be caught most nights at **HBO Workspace**, 733 N. Seward, Tel: 323-903 6099; **Bang Theater**, 457 N. Fairfax Avenue, Tel: 323-653 6886, has a wide range of offerings Thursday–Sunday. Also note **The Laugh Factory** and **Comedy Store** on Sunset Strip (see *page 74*).

Interesting bars

As far back as Rudolph Valentino's day the stars hung out at the **Hollywood Athletic Club** (6525 Hollywood Boulevard, Tel: 323-962 6600) shooting pool, exercising and – mostly – drinking, and today it's still very much more than a bar. And always interesting.

Father's Office (1018 Montana Avenue, Santa Monica, Tel: 310-451 9330) serves different draught beers from 31 taps, with another 40 or so in bottles and cans. **Dublin's Irish Whiskey Pub** (8240 Sunset Boulevard, Tel: 213-656 0100, is a low key sports bar with pool tables and dart boards.

Two chic spots attached to West Hollywood hotels are the **Bar Marmont**, attached to the hotel of that name at 8171 Sunset, Tel: 323-650 0575, and the hard-to-access **Sky Bar** at the newly refurbished Mondrian, Tel: 213-848 6025. Call in advance to get on the list. Similarly chic is the **C Bar**, 8442 Wilshire, Tel: 213-782 8157, where showbizzy agents predominate.

Coffee Houses

Nightly laid-back entertainment can be found in the best coffee houses, a selection of which follows. Occasionally there is a cover charge but usually admission is free. Call to ask about performances.

Try the **Un-Urban Coffee House**, 3301 Pico Boulevard, Santa Monica, Tel: 310-

315 0056; **Petterson's Frisch Röst,** 10019 Venice Boulevard, Tel: 310-839 3359; **Highland Grounds,** 742 North Highland Avenue, Tel: 323-466 1507; **Anastasia's Asylum,** 1028 Wilshire Boulevard, Tel: 310-394 7113; **Moondog Café,** 7160 Melrose, Tel: 323-9236 4604; **Lucy Florence Coffeehouse,** 6541 Santa Monica Boulevard, Tel: 323-463 7585; or **Little Frida's Coffee House,** 8730 Santa Monica Boulevard, Tel: 310-854 5421.

Theaters and Serious Stuff

There's always something going on downtown at the **Music Center,** particularly at the Mark Taper Forum (Tel: 213-972 0700 for ticket info), likewise at the Art Deco **Wiltern Theater,** 3790 Wilshire, Tel: 213-380 5005, and the one-time home of the Oscars, the **Pantages Theater,** 6233 Hollywood Boulevard, Tel: 323-468 1770. The **Tiffany Theater,** 8532 Sunset, Tel: 310-289 2999, is rarely dark.

No summer visitor would dream of overlooking the wide-ranging offerings of the **Hollywood Bowl,** 2301 N. Highland, Tel: 323-850 2000, and lovers of the stage will find a large array of small, experimental theaters. Among the best of these are the MET **Theater,** 1089 N. Oxford, tel: 323-957 1152; the **Matrix Theater Company,** 7657 Melrose, Tel: 323-852 1445; the **Colony Studio Theater,** 1944 Riverside Drive, Silver Lake, Tel: 323-665 3011; and **Tamarind Theater,** 5919 Franklin, Tel: 323-465 7980, whose location alone makes it worth a visit. Consult the weekly papers for schedules.

The stretch between Cole Avenue and Seward Street along Santa Monica Boulevard in Hollywood has come to be known as **Theater Row,** with a dozen theaters, two acting schools, an Italian restaurant and a coffee shop along three blocks. Most of the theaters have less than 50 seats, usually costing under $10, and the *Westside Weekly* reported that you can easily end up sitting next to the person who wrote the play. 'You can walk into one of these little theaters and be blown away by something' says actor Martin Landau. 'These are great training grounds for young actors.'

Where the Stars Hang Out

When 5,000 travel agents came to town for their Los Angeles Convention in late 1998, the *Los Angeles Times* put out a special supplement telling them where to find the stars at night. Some of the places have been well-known celebrity hangouts for a long time, such as the Chateau Marmont's **Marmont Bar** (see *Interesting Bars*), to which short-term residents naturally gravitate. Its spectacular opening in 1995 coincided with Leonardo Di Caprio's birthday party. And nobody would be surprised, of course, to find celebrities at such Beverly Hills hotels as the famous 'Pink Lady' on Sunset, the Regent Beverly Wilshire and the Bel Air.

Harry's Bar at the ABC Entertainment Center in Century City is said to be

The Hollywood Bowl

a favorite of Sean Connery and Geena Davis (their lawyers' offices are nearby). Popular dinner spots for various stars are **Mr Chow's** on North Camden Drive; the back room of **Le Dome** on Sunset; **Pane e Vino** on Beverly Boulevard; **Patina** on Melrose Avenue; and **Little Door,** two blocks west of the Beverly Center, which is so incognito that it doesn't even have a name on the door.

In a different category altogether is the **Westside Billiards Café** in the Beverly Center. Here from 11am to midnight most days, and until 2am on Fridays and Saturdays, pool tables can be rented by the hour and curious spectators can order beer and pizza. Next door is the Hard Rock Café. 'We get people from LA, Hard Rock gets tourists,' says a Westside bar tender.

Calendar of Special Events

JANUARY

Palm Springs Film Festival, Tel: 760- 778 8979
Whale Watch Weekend, **Cabrillo National Monument**, Tel: 619-557 5450
Rose Bowl and Parade, **Pasadena**, Tel: 818-449-ROSE
Martin Luther King Celebration, **Los Angeles**. Parade from 7th Street to King Park, Tel: 562-570 5614

FEBRUARY

LA Bach Festival, Tel: 213-385 1435
Chinese New Year, **Los Angeles**, Tel: 213-617 0396
Date Festival and Riverside County Fair, **Indio**, Tel: 760-863 8247
Festival of Brides, **Los Angeles Convention Center**, Tel: 310-577 7788
Queen Mary Scottish Festival, **Long Beach**, Tel: 562-435 3511

MARCH

Old Pasadena St Patrick's Day Parade, Tel: 818-796 5049
Village Arts Festival, **Palm Springs**, Tel: 818-709 2907

Ocean Beach Kite Festival, Tel: 619-224 0189
Bull Wrestling Contest, **Long Beach**, Tel: 562-436 3661
International Film Festival, **Santa Barbara**, Tel: 805-963 0023
City of **Los Angeles** Marathon, Tel: 310-444 5544

APRIL

Blessing of the Animals, Olvera Street, **Los Angeles**, Tel: 213-628 1274
Old **Encinitas** Street Fair, Tel: 619-943 1950
Borrego Springs Grapefruit Festival, Tel: 619-767 5555
Desert Dixieland Festival, **Palm Springs**, Tel: 760-321-JASS
Toyota Grand Prix, **Long Beach**, Tel: 1-800-752 9524
Point Mugu Air Show, **Point Mugu Air Base**, Tel: 805-989 8786

MAY

Renaissance Pleasure Faire, **Glen Helen**, Tel: 800-52-FAIRE
Ramona Outdoor Play, **Hemet**, Tel: 909-658 3111

Jousting at the Renaissance Faire

Spring Vilage Faire, **Carlsbad**, Tel: 619-931 8400

California Strawberry Festival, **College Park**, Tel: 805-385 7578

JUNE

Score Baja 500 Race, Tel: 818-583 8068

La Jolla Concerts by the Sea, Tel: 619-525 3160

Shipwrecked at the Isthmus, **Catalina**, Tel: 310-510 0303

San Fernando Valley Fair, **LA Equestrian Center**, Tel: 818-557 1600

Wine Festival, **Ojai**, Tel: 800-648 4881

JULY

Jazz in the Park, **Carlsbad**, Tel: 619-434 2904

San Diego Wooden Boat Festival, Tel: 619-226 3446

Pershing Square Summer Conerts, **Los Angeles**, Tel: 213-485 8044

Shakespeare Festival, outside **LA City Hall**, Tel: 213-489 1121

AUGUST

Long Beach Jazz Festival, Tel: 310-562 7794

Ramona Country Fair Days, Tel: 619-789 1484

Taste of **San Pedro**, Point Fermin Park, Tel: 310-832 1357

African Marketplace and Cultural Faire, **Rancho Cienega Park**, Tel: 213-734 1164

SEPTEMBER

Los Angeles County Fair, Tel: 909-623 3111

Uptown **Whittier** Art Walk, Tel: 562-696 2662

Philippine Arts Festival, **San Pedro**, Tel: 213-389 3050

Julian Fall Apple Harvest, Tel: 619-765 1857

Rosarito-Ensenada Fun Bicycle Ride, Tel: 619-583 3001

Rodeo Stampede, **Barstow**, Tel: 619-256 8617

OCTOBER

South Bay Greek Festival, **Redondo**, Tel: 310-540 2434

Calabasas Pumpkin Festival, **Agoura**, Tel: 818-222 5680

Lithuanian Fair, St Casimir Church, **Los Angeles**, Tel: 818- 564 7354

West Hollywood Halloween Carnival, Tel: 323-848 6547

California Avocado Festival, **Carpinteria**, Tel: 805-684 0038

NOVEMBER

Palm Desert Golf Cart Parade, Tel: 800-873 2428

Doo Dah Parade, **Pasadena**, Tel: 626-449 3689

Hollywood Christmas Parade, Tel: 323-469 2337

Death Valley '49er Encampment, **Furnace Creek**, Tel: 619-254 2047

DECEMBER

Tree Lighting at **Queen Mary**, Tel: (562) 435-3511

Griffith Park Winter Celebration, Tel: 213-469 8311

Palm Springs Celebrity Golf Classic, Tel: 760-322 1769

Renenactment of Battle of San Pasqual, **Escondido**, Tel: 619-489 0076

Practical Information

GETTING THERE

By Air

Sixty major airlines serve **Los Angeles International Airport** (LAX). Only domestic carriers operate to and from **San Diego airport** from which SDTC bus No 2 runs regularly to downtown. **Santa Barbara's airport** is located 8 miles north of downtown. Smaller airports in the region include Burbank, Ontario, Palm Springs, Palm Desert, and John Wayne, the Orange County airport in Santa Ana, which is the nearest to Disneyland.

Right outside the main arrival building at LAX are information booths manned by helpful personnel who will tell you the best route to where you are going. A free shuttle bus runs to a city bus station about 1 mile away and from here RTD buses and Santa Monica Big Blue Buses run to most parts of the city. Schedules are posted. It is possible, therefore, to get to almost anywhere in LA County for under a couple of bucks. Local authorities have been trying to cut down on the multitude of shuttle services operating out of the airport. Still running are: Prime Time Shuttle, Tel: 800-REDVANS; Super Shuttle, Tel: 800-554 3146; and LA Xpress, Tel: 310-337 0990. These will take you from the airport to your door and vice versa.

By Rail

The Coast Starlight connects Los Angeles with San Francisco, Portland and Oregon along the magnificent California coastline. In LA, all trains arrive at Amtrak's downtown **Union Station**, a historic landmark, from which there is a regular service to northern and southern California. Two trans-continental trains a day run to and from Chicago (a 2-day journey) with an additional train operating twice a week. For schedules and further information call 1-800-USA-RAIL.

By Road

Greyhound Trailways operates a nationwide bus service with depots in downtown **Los Angeles** (Los Angeles and 6th streets, Tel: 213-629 8400) and in Hollywood (1409 Vine Street, Tel: 323-466 6381). In **San Diego**, Greyhound Trailways' depot is at 120 West Broadway, Tel: 619-239 3636. The **Palm Springs** bus depot is located at 311 North Indian Canyon Drive, Tel: 619-325 2053. **Santa Barbara** Greyhound: Tel: 805-966 3962 for information.

The major highways to the north are US Highway 101 (Ventura and Hollywood freeways); State Highway 1 (the Pacific Coast Highway which begins in San Diego), both of which run to San

Francisco and further north; and Interstate 5 (Golden State and Santa Ana freeways) between San Diego, LA, Sacramento and Seattle. Eastwards, Interstate 10 (San Bernadino and Santa Monica freeways) runs from Santa Monica all the way to Florida, passing through Houston and New Orleans.

TRAVEL ESSENTIALS

When to Visit/Weather

Southern California has uniformly pleasant weather most of the year. Some rain can be expected in winter and early spring, but never snow, and rarely will daytime temperatures drop below 17°C (60°F) even in January. Midsummer can be scorching and visitors may be surprised by the characteristic morning fog. Spring and fall are balmy, beaches uncrowded and Disneyland lines (slightly) shorter.

Visas

Canadians and Mexican citizens with border passports do not require passports or visas. Britons need passports but not visas if entering direct from Britain. All other foreigners must have both. Do not bring agricultural products into California.

Clothing

Casual wear like shorts and T-shirts are acceptable almost everywhere, although a few restaurants require jackets and ties for men. Sweaters may be needed for cooler evenings and heavier coats in winter.

Electricity

The standard rating is 110V.

Time Zones

Southern California is on Pacific Time, 3 hours behind New York, 8 hours behind London, 16 hours behind Tokyo. Daylight Savings Time begins the first Sunday in April, and ends the last Sunday in October.

GETTING ACQUAINTED

Geography and Population

Measured by its 30 million population, California is America's biggest state but physically it is in third place, stretching about 600 miles between the Mexican and Oregon borders. Strictly speaking then, 'Southern California' should be the bottom half of this enormous land mass but in practice it has come to mean everything south of San Luis Obispo and Bakersfield, so it is only the bottom third. The state's two biggest cities, San Diego and Los Angeles, fall within this area with LA having become so dominant it

License to thrill

is, to the chagrin of its neighbors, almost a synonym for 'Southern California.'

Greater Los Angeles (pop: 8½ million), bordered by mountains to the northeast and north, includes miles of coastline and is the central destination in Southern California. In the east it reaches into the desert, stretches about halfway to Santa Barbara in the north, and to the border of San Diego County in the south. Many of the communities within this area – Santa Monica, Beverly Hills, West Hollywood, Pasadena, Long Beach – are themselves incorporated cities in their own right. RTD buses run all the way to the borders of Los Angeles County, which also includes Anaheim, home of Disneyland.

Money Matters

Dollar bills of all denominations ($1, 5, 10, 20, 50, 100) confusingly are all green. Two-dollar bills exist but are unpopular and rare; ditto for 50¢ and $1 coins (except in Reno and Las Vegas). Major **credit cards** are accepted in larger stores and in most hotels and restaurants. **Cash machines** (ATMs) exist outside branches of

most major banks, some of which accept transactions in cards from other banks. Large supermarket chains often have cash machines from which money can be obtained using credit cards.

Apart from Bank of America branches, very few banks exchange **foreign currency** away from the airport. This is best done at American Express branches (consult phone book for addresses). Bring your passport.

Should your credit card be **stolen**, call American Express at 1-800-528 2121 or Discover card at 1-800-858 5588. For Mastercard or Visa contact your bank. For lost or stolen travelers' checks call Amex 1-800-221 7282; Bank America 1-800-227 3460; Visa 1-800-227 6811.

GETTING AROUND
Taxis and Buses

Except for short trips, taxis are not a preferred method of travel in Los Angeles because of the distances to be covered. Some taxi companies are: **Yellow Cab**, Tel: 213-808 1000, **United Independent**, Tel: 213-462 1088 and **Checker**, Tel: 310-330 3730. Fares begin at about $2, plus about $1.60 for each additional mile. (It is about 20 miles from downtown to the coast). RTD buses are slow but reliable, operate on most major cross streets and run 24 hours a day (RTD info: Tel: 213-626 4455). A long-range public transportation plan for the city has so far produced the Metro Blue Line between downtown LA and Long Beach.

Car Rentals

When you visit places other than LA, a car will prove almost invaluable, although Santa Barbara and Palm Springs are easily accessible to the pedestrian. Car rentals in Los Angeles and San Diego are relatively inexpensive, beginning at about

Balmy beach days

$30 per day plus 21¢ per mile after the first 150 miles. Some of the bigger companies – Avis, Budget, Hertz and National – operate in both cities. Consult the *Yellow Pages* for rental companies near to you.

HOURS AND HOLIDAYS
Business Hours

A regular 9am-5pm day is commonplace, but many of the shopping malls stay open until 9pm and some supermarkets often operate around the clock. A few banks stay open beyond their usual 3pm closing on Friday, and open Saturday mornings.

Public Holidays

Banks and most federal, state and municipal offices are closed on the following holidays:

January:	**New Year's Day**
	Martin Luther King Day
February:	**President's Day**
March/April:	**Easter Sunday**
May:	**Memorial Day**
July 4:	**Independence Day**
September:	**Labor Day**
November:	**Thanksgiving** (2 days)
December:	**Christmas Day**

Additional holidays observed by many businesses and banks include:

Lincoln's Birthday (February 12); **Good Friday**; **Columbus Day** (second Monday in October) and **Veterans' Day** (November 11).

ACCOMMODATION

Los Angeles is a sprawling city and so it pays to make an early decision on where you want stay. Whether you own (or rent) a car obviously will make a difference; downtown parking costs, for example, are extremely high. It's likely that most of your time will be spent west of downtown – in the Hollywood area or on the coast. There are plenty of choices, but reservations are highly recommended; tourism is an all-year business. Listed (1-800) numbers are charge-free central reservation offices. $ = under $100; $$ = under $200; $$$ = above $200. Prices are for a double room.

Downtown

BEST WESTERN EXECUTIVE MOTOR INN
603 South New Hampshire Avenue
Tel: 213-385 4444 or 1-800-528 1234
All rooms have refrigerators and cable TV. There's a laundromat and swimming pool on the premises and the airport bus stops here. *$*

CHANCELLOR HOTEL AND RESIDENCE
3191 West 7th Street
Tel: 213-383 1183
Recreation room, swimming pool and free parking are features of this moderately priced hotel. *$*

HOLIDAY INN DOWNTOWN
750 Garland Avenue
Tel: 213-628 5242 or 1-800-465 4329
All rooms have cable TV and there is also a restaurant, bar and swimming pool. This is a stop along the airport bus route. *$*

WILSHIRE ROYALE HOTEL
2619 Wilshire Boulevard
Tel: 213-387 5311 or 1-800-421 8072
Within easy reach of the Convention Center, the hotel has a restaurant, coffee shop, pool, tennis, laundromat and offers a baby-sitting service. *$*

BANANA BUNGALOW
2775 Cahuenga Boulevard
Tel: 1-800-4-HOSTEL
Backpackers' paradise. Pool, restaurant, exercise room. *$*

THE NEW OTANI
120 S Los Angeles Street
Tel: 213-629 1200 or 1-800-421 8795
Tranquil and charming Japanese garden above the bustle of a shopping arcade with restaurants and bars. On the edge of Japantown. *$$*

HYATT REGENCY
701 South Hope Street
Tel: 213-683 1234 or 1-800-233 1244
Centrally located, an easy walk from the Jewelry Mart, the Hyatt has restaurants, jacuzzi, and offers baby-sitting services. *$$*

MAYFAIR HOTEL
1256 West 7th Street
Tel: 213-484 9789 or 1-800-821 8682
Pickford and Barrymore came to lunch in the 1930s. The old-time elegance has been retained after a $40 million renovation. *$$*

KAWADA HOTEL
200 South Hill Street
Tel: 213-621 4455
The hotel restaurant has an earthquake theme. *$$*

WESTIN BONAVENTURE
404 South Figueroa Avenue
Tel: 213-624 1000 or 1-800-228 3000
Its landmark silvered towers are topped with a revolving rooftop restaurant and the hotel's spacious interior is a joy to behold. *$$$*

THE REGAL BILTMORE
506 South Grand Avenue
Tel: 213-624 1011 or 1-800-421 8000
With its classic lobby and longtime reputation for style and luxury, this well-known hotel is also right in the center of things. *$$$*

HOTEL INTER CONTINENTAL
251 South Olive
Tel: 213-617 3300
Luxury hotel beside the California Plaza, opposite MOCA. *$$$*

MIYAKO INN & SPA
328 East 1st Street
Tel/fax: 213-617 2000 or phone 1-800-228 6596
Japanese style with mineral baths, jacuzzis, Shiatsu massage, karaoke bar. *$$$*

San Diego trolley

The Hollywood Area

DUNES SUNSET MOTEL
5625 Sunset Boulevard
Tel: 323-467 5171 or 1-800-452 3863
Not far from the Chinese Theater and other attractions, it has a restaurant, bar, free parking and easy access to the airport bus. *$*

THE MAGIC HOTEL
7025 Franklin
Tel: 323-851 0800
Has the same owners as the nearby Magic Castle and its lobby is adorned with posters of famous magicians. There's a swimming pool, laundromat and free parking. *$*

Westin Bonaventure

ALTA CIENEGA MOTEL
1005 North La Cienega
Tel: 310-652 5797
Inexpensive, no frills and rumored to have hosted the Doors, including Jim Morrison. *$*

ACADEMY HOTEL
1621 N McCadden Place
Tel: 213-465 1191
A small budget hotel with friendly staff near to most of Hollywood's main attractions. *$*

HOLLOWAY MOTEL
8465 Santa Monica Boulevard
Tel/Fax: 323-654 2454
Friendly place with free breakfast. *$*

PARK SUNSET HOTEL
8462 Sunset Boulevard
Tel: 323-654 6470 or 1-800-821 3660
Fax: 323-654 5918
Within walking distance of the Strip. Pool, sundeck. *$*

FAIRFAX MOTEL
913 North Fairfax Avenue
Tel: 323-654 5570
Small, inexpensive and under the same ownerships since the 1950s. *$*

RAMADA WEST HOLLYWOOD
8585 Santa Monica Boulevard
Tel: 310-652 6400 or 1-800-845 8585
Fax: 310-652 2135
Pool, restaurants, multilingual staff. *$$*

LE REVE HOTEL
8822 Cynthia Street
Tel: 310-854 1114 or 1-800-835 7997
Fax: 310-657 2623
Intimate, country-style hotel with suites equipped with fireplaces, balconies and kitchenettes. Rooftop pool, lush gardens, fitness center. *$$*

THE ARGYLE
8358 Sunset Boulevard
Tel: 310-654 7100 or 1-800-225 2637
Fax: 310-654 9287
Formerly the renowned Art Deco St James Club on Sunset Strip. Health spa and pool with panoramic city views. *$$*

HYATT WEST HOLLYWOOD
8401 Sunset Boulevard
Tel: 323-656 1234 or 1-800-233 1234
Fax: 232-650 7024
Rooftop pool, restaurants, multilingual staff. *$$*

HOLLYWOOD ROOSEVELT
7000 Hollywood Boulevard
Tel: 323-466 7000 or 1-800-338 7256
Legendary home of first Oscars. Its downstairs pool is palm-fringed, the restaurant is Art Deco style and there's an exhibit of 'old Hollywood' on the mezzanine floor. *$$*

BEST WESTERN HOLLYWOOD PLAZA INN
2011 North Highland Avenue
Tel: 323-851 1800 or 1-800-232 4353
Near Hollywood Bowl, it has valuable free parking space, plus swimming pool and laundromat. *$$*

BEVERLY GARLAND
4222 Vineland Avenue

The Regal Biltmore Hotel

Tel: 818-980 8000 or 1-800-654 2000
Near Universal Studios, it has restaurant, bar, pool and tennis courts. *$$*

HOLIDAY INN HOLLYWOOD
1755 North Highland Avenue
Tel: 323-462 7181 or 1-800-465 4329
Centrally located near the Hollywood Bowl, it has a rooftop restaurant, swimming pool and free parking. *$$*

SAN VICENTE INN
845 North San Vicente
Tel: 310-854 6915
Fax: 310-289 5929
Pool, sauna. Caters mainly to a gay clientele. *$$*

HOLLYWOOD METROPOLITAN
5825 Sunset Boulevard
Tel: 213-962 5800
Central for entertainment district. Penthouse restaurant. *$$*

MONDRIAN HOTEL
8440 Sunset Boulevard
Tel: 323-650 8999 or 1-800-424 4443
Fax: 323-650 5215
This chic, art-filled hotel with swimming pool and outdoor terrace/bar is a popular rendezvous for movie types. *$$$*

LE MONTROSE SUITE HOTEL
900 Hammond Street
Tel: 310-855 1115 or 1-800-776 0666
Fax: 310-657 9192
Luxury all-suite hideaway with a $2 million art collection. Rooftop pool, tennis court, fitness center. *$$$*

BEL AGE HOTEL
1020 North San Vicente Boulevard
Tel: 310-854 1111 or 1-800-424 4443
Fax: 310-854 0926
There's classy art everywhere and even the bathrooms have TV. Swimming pool and popular business restaurant. *$$$*

Beverly Hills

BEVERLY REEVES B&B
120 South Reeves Drive
Tel: 310-271 3006
Two blocks from Wilshire and Rodeo on quiet, tree-lined street. *$*

BEVERLY HOUSE HOTEL
140 South Lasky Drive
Tel: 310-271 2145 or 1-800-432 5544
Fax: 310-276 8431
European-style B&B, centrally situated. *$$*

BEVERLY HILLS INN
125 South Spalding Drive
Tel: 1-800-463 4466
Fax: 310-278 1728
Small boutique hotel with free full breakfast, pool, sauna. *$$*

BEVERLY HILLS HOTEL
9641 Sunset Boulevard
Tel: 310-276 2251 or 1-800-283-8885
Fax: 310-887 2887
Luxury bungalows discreetly located in landscaped grounds. Cellular phones almost *de rigueur* around swimming pool. Stars in famous Polo Lounge don't balk at $5 tariff for a glass of orange juice. *$$$*

REGENT BEVERLY WILSHIRE
9500 Wilshire Boulevard
Tel: 310-275 5200 or 1-800-421 4354
Just a few steps from the shopping along Rodeo Drive and the other expensive delights of Beverly Hills. *$$$*

BEVERLY HILTON
9876 Wilshire Boulevard
Tel: 310-274 7777 or 1-800-445 8667
Fax: 310-859 9011
In its own grounds close to where Wilshire and Santa Monica boulevards intersect and thus a short walk from Rodeo Drive. *$$$*

HOTEL BEL AIR
701 Stone Canyon Road
Tel: 310-472 1211 or 1-800-648 4097

Some consider this the most charming hotel in the region. An elegantly landscaped hideaway in its own grounds with stream and terrace restaurant. $$$

PENINSULA
9882 Little Santa Monica Boulevard
Tel: 310-551 2888 or 1-800-462 7899
Fax: 310-788 2319
Luxurious terrace suites plus 16 villas in landscaped garden. $$$

BEVERLY PRESCOTT
12245 Beverwill Drive
Tel: 310-277 2800 or 1-800-421 3212
Fax: 310-203 9537
Elegantly furnished rooms with private balconies that overlook an attractive pool in palm-fringed gardens. $$$

BEVERLY RODEO
360 North Rodeo Drive
Tel: 310-273 0300 or 1-800-356 7575
Fax: 310-859 8730
In the midst of all the classy shops, with the only sidewalk restaurant on the famous shopping street. $$$

Pasadena

PASADENA HOTEL
76 North Fair Oaks Avenue
Tel: 626-793 9313
Small, very central. $$

RITZ CARLTON HUNTINGTON
140 South Oak Knoll
Tel: 818-568 3900
Super de luxe landmark with original 1907 ballroom. $$$

Santa Monica/Malibu/Catalina

SANTA MONICA PICO TRAVELODGE
3102 Pico Boulevard
Tel: 310-450 5766 or 1-800-231 7679
Fax: 310-450 8843
Near the beach, kitchen units, laundromat, free breakfast and free parking. $

SANTA MONICA BEACH TRAVEL LODGE
1525 Ocean Avenue
Tel: 310-451 0761 or 1-800-255 3050
Fax: 310-393 5311
Close to beach and shopping, it has swimming pool, free parking. $$

BAYVIEW PLAZA HOTEL
530 Pico Boulevard
Tel: 310-399 9344 or 1-800-465 4329
Fax: 310-399 2504
Near the beach, it has restaurants, bar, laundromat and free parking. $$

HOTEL CARMEL
201 Broadway
Tel: 310-451 2469 or 1-800-445 8695
Fax: 310-393 4180
Some rooms have view of the ocean, two blocks away. $$

BAYSIDE HOTEL
2001 Ocean Avenue, Santa Monica
Tel: 310-396 6000
Overlooks the ocean. $$

CAL MAR HOTEL SUITES
220 California Avenue
Tel: 310-395 5555
On a quiet residential street two blocks from the ocean. Pool, kitchens. $$

MARINA PACIFIC HOTEL & SUITES
1697 Pacific Avenue, Venice
Tel: 310-452 1111 or 1-800-421 8151
Adjoins famous boardwalk beside the ocean. Outdoor sidewalk café. $$

THE GEORGIAN HOTEL
1415 Ocean Avenue, Santa Monica
Tel: 310-395 0945
Elegant Art Deco place overlooking the ocean. $$

SHANGRI-LA HOTEL
1301 Ocean Avenue
Tel: 310-394 2791 or 1-800-345-STAY
Fax: 310-451 3351
Famous for its Art Deco, it overlooks the clifftop park and ocean; laundry, free parking, airport bus. $$

MIRAMAR-SHERATON
101 Wilshire Boulevard
Tel: 310-567-7777 or 1-800-325 3535
Fax: 310-458-7912
Lovely tropical garden setting with enormous trees, on the site of the home of the city's founder. Well equipped with restaurants and bars, it has a swimming pool and baby-sitting facilities. $$

MALIBU COUNTRY INN
6506 Westward Beach Road
Tel: 310-457 9622
Overlooking the ocean, with pool and baby-sitting facilities. *$$*

HOTEL ST LAUREN
PO Box 2166, Avalon, Catalina
Tel: 310-510 2299 or 1-800-645 2478
Charming Victorian-style place built in 1987. Rooftop patio. *$$*

LOEWS SANTA MONICA BEACH HOTEL
1700 Ocean Avenue
Tel: 310-458 6700 or 1-800-223 0888
Fax: 310-458 6761
The town's first new luxury hotel for many years, it overlooks the beach near the pier and has restaurants, bar, pool and laundromat. *$$$*

MALIBU BEACH INN
22878 Pacific Coast Highway
Tel: 310-456 6444
Close to Malibu Pier, its rooms have balconies overlooking the beach. There's a VCR and personal safe in each room. *$$$*

SNUG HARBOR INN
Avalon, Catalina Island
Tel: 310-510 1520
Renovated (renamed) century-old hotel. *$$$*

Catalina Island Accommodations, Tel: 310-510 3000.

San Fernando Valley

SHERATON UNIVERSAL
333 Universal Terrace Parkway,
Universal City
Tel: 818-980 1212 or 1-800 325 3535
Fax: 818-985 4980
Pool, whirlpool, health club. Free shuttle to nearby Universal Studio tour and CityWalk. *$$*

Santa Barbara

FRANCISCAN INN
109 Bath Street
Tel: 805-963 8845
At the beach; has health club, swimming pool and tennis courts. *$*

VILLA ROSA
15 Chapala Avenue
Tel: 805-966 0851
Located at the beach, the Villa Rosa has a swimming pool and spa. *$$*

EL ENCANTO
1900 Lasuen Street
Tel: 805-687 5000
In town; restaurant, swimming pool, tennis. *$$*

THE UPHAM
1404 De La Vina
Tel: 805-962 0058
The last of Santa Barbara's century-old hotels, operated as a classy B&B set around a delightful garden. *$$*

OJAI VALLEY INN & SPA
Tel: 1-800-422 6524
Tennis, swimming, golf, excercise classes, good food. *$$$*

Palm Springs

ASA CODY
175 S Cahuila Road
Tel: 619-320 9246
Founded by Buffalo Bill's niece; attractive, airy suites around pool. *$*

VILLA ROYALE
1620 Indian Trail
Tel: 619-327 2314
Lovely hideaway, charming courtyards, pool; suites decorated in styles of many different countries. *$$*

THE WILLOWS
Tahquitz Canyonway
Tel: 760-320 0771

Hotel del Coronado

Nestling against Mount Jacinto, with palm-fringed pool and two-story waterfall. *$$$*

INGLESIDE INN
2000 Ramon at Belardo
Tel: 619-325 0046
Greta Garbo slept here; garden, antiques, pool, fine restaurant. *$$$*

San Diego

DAYS INN DOWNTOWN
1449 Ninth Avenue
Tel: 619-239 9113 or 1-800-325 2525
Fax: 619-232 9019
Central near shops with shuttle bus and swimming pool. *$*

HORTON GRAND HOTEL
311 Island Avenue
Tel: 619-544 1886 or 1-800-542 1886
Fax: 619-239 3823
Victorian landmark in Gaslamp district. Rooms with fireplaces. Restaurant, 'traditional tea'. *$$*

HOLIDAY INN ON THE BAY
1355 North Harbor Drive
Tel: 619-232 3861 or 1-800-877 8920
Fax: 619-232 3951
Very central.With four restaurants and pool. *$$*

HOTEL DEL CORONADO
150 Orange Avenue, Coronado
Tel: 619-435 6611 or 1-800 HOTEL DEL
World-famous Victorian-era landmark; tennis court and pool. *$$$*

Bed and Breakfast

Hundreds of B&Bs are listed in the $4 guide produced by the California Association of B&B Inns, 2715 Porter St, So-

quel, CA 95073. Or contact **US Bed &** **Breakfast**, Tel: 1-800-US B-AND-B, fo B&B information nationwide.

HEALTH AND EMERGENCIES
Medical Services

The *Yellow Pages* list many doctors, hospitals and pharmacists. Three drugstore chains have branches all over California **Rexall**, **Sav-On** and **Thrifty**, with some branches open 24 hours. In LA, the down town branch of **Horton & Converse**, 73: South Figueroa, Tel: 213-623 2838 i open until 7pm weekdays and its branch at 11600 Wilshire Boulevard, Tel: 310 478 0801 remains open until 2am.

Large hospitals are **Cedars-Sinai Medi cal Center**, 8700 Beverly Boulevard, Tel 310-855 5000; **Hollywood Presbyterian Medical** Center, 1300 North Vermon Avenue, Tel: 213-413 3000; UCLA, 1083: Le Conte Avenue, Tel: 310-825 9111.

In **Palm Springs**, call 619-323 8181 for fire or medical aid. The Desert Hospi tal is at 1150 Indian Canyon Drive, Tel 619-323 6100. In **San Diego**, a usefu number might be the Medical Society Re ferral Service, Tel: 619-565 8181.

COMMUNICATIONS AND NEWS
Media

There are at least a score of daily news papers in Southern California. The daily *Los Angeles Times* blankets the regior with different editions and one of the sec tions in its fat Sunday edition is a maga zine-type calendar with complete listings of just about all activities. The otherwise soporific *LA Weekly* is good for loca listings, as is its free and more interest ing) rival the *Reader*. More than 60 radic stations and at least 30 television stations broadcast in the Los Angeles area alone.

Telephone/Fax

Unless otherwise stated the Los Angeles prefix is **213**. The western section of the city (ie most of the coastal area from Ma rina del Ray to Malibu and inland to La Cienega Boulevard) is now in the **310** area. The eastern section (ie the San Fernando and San Gabriel valleys) is in the

818 area. All out-of-your-area codes require dialing **1** first. The area code for San Diego is **619**; for Santa Barbara **805**; for Palm Springs **619**.

To dial other countries (Canada follows the US system), first dial the international access code **011**, then the country code: **Australia** (61); **France** (33); **Germany** (49); **Italy** (39); **Japan** (81); **Mexico** (52); **Spain** (34); **United Kingdom** (44). If using a US credit phone card, dial the company's access number below, then 01, then the country code. Sprint, Tel: 10333; AT&T, Tel: 10288.

Fax machines are available in most hotels. They can also be found in many of the ubiquitous photo-copying places.

USEFUL INFORMATION

Tours

Los Angeles

GRAYLINE TOURS, Tel: 816-333 2577. Over 25 tours in the city and region.
GRAVELINE TOURS, Tel: 323-469 4149. Visit numerous ghoulish sites.
THE NEXT STAGE TOURS, PO Box 1065, Pasadena, Tel: 626-577 7880. Insomniacs, lovers of secret gardens, icons of LA, etc.
OFF 'N RUNNING, Tel: 310-246 1418; outside LA Tel: 1-800-523 8687. Excercise while you sightsee.
GOOGIE TOURS, Tel: 213-980 3480. Urban archaeologist John English explores 'LA's atomic age landmarks'.
LOS ANGELES CONSERVANCY, Tel: 213-623 2489. Downtown, old movie theaters, other landmarks.

Movie and TV Tours

UNIVERSAL STUDIOS, 3900 Lankershim Boulevard, Universal City, Tel: 818-508 9600. Daily 9am–6.30pm in winter, 8am–10pm in summer.
PARAMOUNT PICTURES, 860 North Gower, Tel: 213-956 6675. 11am and 2pm; no reservations.
BURBANK STUDIO TOUR, Warner-Lorimar studios, 4000 Warner Boulevard, Burbank, Tel: 818-954 1744. Monday–Friday 10am and 2pm; reservations essential.

A daily schedule of which movies are being shot on the city streets is available each morning from the **LA Film and Video Permit Office**, 6922 Hollywood Boulevard. **Audiences Unlimited** (5746 Sunset Boulevard, Tel: 818-506 0043), **CBS** (7800 Beverly Boulevard, Tel: 213-852 2458) and **NBC** (300 Alameda Avenue, Burbank, Tel: 818-840 3538) give out free tickets every day for the taping of TV shows.

Santa Barbara

COURTHOUSE TOURS, Tel: 805-962 6464. Saturday–Tuesday 2pm; Wednesday and Friday 10.30am.
TOURING TAXI OF SANTA BARBARA, Tel: 805-962 2344.
SANTA BARBARA DETOURS, Tel: 805-684 6050.
CAPTAIN DON'S HARBOR TOURS, Tel: 805-969 5217.

Palm Springs

DESERT ADVENTURES, Tel: 619-324 5337.
DREAM FLIGHTS, Tel: 1-800-933 9628. Balloon trips.
COVERED WAGON TOURS OF COACHELLA VALLEY, Tel: 760-347 2161.

San Diego

OLD TOWN TROLLEY TOURS, 2115 Kurtz, Tel: 619-298 8687. 90-minute tours regularly between 9am and dusk.
GRAY LINE TOURS, 1775 Hancock, Tel: 619-491 0011. Fifteen itineraries complete with hotel pick-ups.
DAYTRIPPER TOURS, 3607 Fifth Avenue, Tel: 619-299 5777. Group sightseeing of the area, including Mexico.
BAJA CALIFORNIA TOURS, La Jolla, Tel: 619-454 7166, Fax: 619-454 2703.

Museums

Los Angeles

ARMAND HAMMER MUSEUM OF ART AND CULTURE, 10899 Wilshire Boulevard, Tel: 310-443 7000. Wednesday–Monday noon–7pm, free on Thursday.
AUTRY MUSEUM OF WESTERN HERITAGE, Griffith Park at the junction of the Golden State and Ventura freeways, Tel: 213-667 2000. Tuesday–Sunday 10am–5pm. The Old West, in fact and fiction. MTA bus No 97 stops outside.

CALIFORNIA SCIENCE CENTER, Exposition Park, Tel: 213-724 3623. Daily 10am–5pm. Slick, wonderfully interactive educational and entertaining exhibits.

GEORGE C PAGE MUSEUM OF LA BREA DISCOVERIES, 5801 Wilshire Boulevard, Tel: 323-934 7243. Tuesday–Sunday 10am–5pm.

GETTY CENTER, NW of Sunset Boulevard and I-405 at Brentwood, Tel: 310-440 7300. Tuesday and Wednesday 10am–7pm, Thursday and Friday 10am–9pm, weekends 10am–6pm. Free ($5 parking; reservation essential). MTA bus info: 1-800-266 6883; Blue Bus: 310-452 5444.

GRIFFITHS PARK, Tel: 213-664 1191 for times of the planetarium and laser shows; Tel: 213-626 4455 for DASH schedule. Tel: 213-410 1062 for Greek Theater schedule.

HOLLYWOOD ENTERTAINMENT MUSEUM, 7021 Hollywood Boulevard, Tel: 213-465 7900. Tuesday–Sunday 10am–6pm. Movie history, fashion, Foley sound and the famous *Cheers* bar.

HUNTINGTON ART GALLERY, 1151 Oxford Road, San Marino, Tel: 818-405 2141. Tuesday–Friday noon–4.30pm, weekends 10.30am–4.30pm.

JAPANESE NATIONAL MUSEUM, 369 First Street, Tel: 213-625 0414. New museum opening early 1999.

LOS ANGELES COUNTY MUSEUM OF ART, 5905 Wilshire Boulevard, Tel: 213-857 6111. Tuesday–Friday 10am–5pm. Five buildings covering pre-history to the present day.

MUSEUM OF CONTEMPORARY ART, 250 South Grand Avenue, Tel: 213-621 2766. Friday–Wednesday 11am–8pm, Thursday 1–6pm.

MUSEUM OF TOLERANCE, 9786 West Pico Boulevard, Tel: 310-553 8043. Monday–Thursday 10am–4pm, Friday 10am–3pm.

MUSEUM OF TV AND RADIO, 465 North Beverly Drive, Tel: 310-786 1000. Wednesday–Sunday noon–5pm, until 9pm Thursday. 75,000 TV and radio programs and commercials.

SKIRBALL CULTURAL CENTER, Sepulveda Pass near Getty Center Drive, Tel: 310-440 4500. Tuesday–Saturday noon–5pm, Sunday 11am–5pm. Jewish culture, biblical archaeology.

SOUTHWEST MUSEUM, 234 Museum Drive, Tel: 323-221 2164. Tuesday–Sunday 10am–5pm. Native American culture.

Santa Barbara

HISTORICAL MUSEUM, 136 East de la Guerra, Tel: 805 966 1601. Tuesday–Saturday 10am–5pm, Sunday noon–5pm.

MUSEUM OF ART, 1130 State Street, Tel: 805-963 4364. Tuesday, Wednesday, Friday and Saturday 11am–5pm; Thursday 11am–9pm; Sunday noon–5pm.

MUSEUM OF NATURAL HISTORY, 2559 Puesta del Sol Road, Tel: 805-682 4711. Monday–Saturday 10am–5pm, Sunday noon–5pm.

Palm Springs

HISTORICAL SOCIETY MUSEUM, 77885 Montezuma, Tel: 760-564 1283. Tuesday–Saturday 10am–2pm.

PALM SPRINGS AIR MUSEUM, 7745 North Gene Autry Trail, Tel: 619-778 6262. Vast collection of vintage planes, mostly from World War II.

PALM SPRINGS DESERT MUSEUM, 101 Museum Drive, Tel: 619-325 7186. Tuesday–Sunday 10am–5pm, until 8pm Friday.

San Diego

BALBOA PARK. Ten museums offer an $18 pass good for admission to all of them.

FIREHOUSE MUSEUM, 1572 Columbia Street, Tel: 619-232 3473. Wednesday–Friday 10am–2pm, Saturday and Sunday 10am–4pm.

MARITIME MUSEUM, 1306 North Harbor Drive, Tel: 619-234 9153. Daily 9am–8pm.

MUSEUM OF CONTEMPORARY ART, 700 Prospect Street, La Jolla, Tel: 619-454 3541. Tuesday–Saturday 10am–5pm, Sunday noon–5pm.

SCRIPPS AQUARIUM MUSEUM, La Jolla, Tel: 619-534 3474. Daily 9am–5pm.

SPORTS

April opens LA's baseball season at both **Dodger Stadium** in Elysian Park (Tel: 213-224 1500) and **Anaheim Stadium** (Tel: 714-937 7200), home base of the Angels. The San Diego Padres play at

Horses for hire

vard. Both are open until 5pm every day but Sunday, and both have a large selection of free brochures, leaflets, maps etc.

In **Santa Barbara,** the Visitor Information Centers are at Santa Barbara Street and Stearns Wharf, and 504 State Street, Tel: 805-965 3023. The **Palm Springs** Tourist Office dispenses information via 1-800-34-SPRINGS, or at the Municipal Airport Terminal, Tel: 619-327 8411. The **San Diego** Convention & Visitors Bureau is at 1200 Third Avenue, Tel: 619-232 3101.

San Diego Jack Murphy Stadium (Tel: 619-283 4494), which is also the home-ground for football games of the *San Diego Chargers*.

The USC's (university) football team plays at the **Los Angeles Coliseum**, 3911 South Figueroa Avenue (Tel: 213-747 7111). USC's rival, UCLA, can be found at **Pasadena's Rose Bowl** (Tel: 310-499-ROSE). Adjoining the Coliseum is the **Los Angeles Sports Arena**, Tel: 213-748 0500) where the *Clippers* play pro-basketball sometimes against the *Lakers* whose home base is the **Forum,** Manchester and Prairie boulevards in Inglewood (Tel: 310-419 3100). The Forum also hosts the *Kings*, LA's topnotch ice hockey team (for tickets call: 714-937 6767).

Hollywood Park, 1050 South Prairie, Inglewood, Tel: 310-419 1500, hosts thoroughbred racing April–July and harness racing August–December; **Santa Anita Park**, Huntington Drive, Arcadia, Tel: 213-574 7223 hosts thoroughbred racing December–April and October–November; and the **Del Mar Track,** Via de la Valle, Del Mar, Tel: 619-299 1340, has a season from mid-July to early September.

USEFUL ADDRESSES

Tourist Information

The **Los Angeles Convention & Visitors Bureau** has an office downtown at 695 South Figueroa Street, Tel: 213-689 8822, and a satellite office in the Janes Building, behind 6541 Hollywood Boule-

FURTHER READING

Beverly Hills: Inside the Golden Ghetto by Walter Wagner, Grossett & Dunlap, 1976.

The Big Picture: Murals of Los Angeles by Melba Levick and Stanley Young, Thames & Hudson, 1988.

California's Black Pioneers by Kenneth G Goode, McNally & Loftin,1976.

California Wildlife Reviewing Guide, by Jeanne L. Clarke, Falcon Press, 1996.

Encyclopedia of City and Country, by Dale & Leonard Pitt, University of Cal Press, 1997.

LA Follies by Sam Hall Kaplan, Cityscape Press, 1989.

LA Shortcuts by Brian Roberts and Richard Schwadel, Red Car Press, 1989.

Moviegoers Guide to Hollywood, The by Richard Alleman, Harper & Row, 1985.

Raymond Chandler's Los Angeles by Elizabeth Ward and Alain Silver, Overlook Press, 1989.

Southern California: An Island on the Land by Carey McWilliams, Peregrine Smith, 1973.

This is Hollywood by Ken Schessler, Universal Books, 1992.

The Ultimate Hollywood Tour Book by William. A Gordon, North Ridge Books, 1994.

Maps

Thomas Bros Maps: Los Angeles County. Every street listed and located. Available in any bookstore.

Art & Photo Credits

Photography	Doug Traverso *and*
Pages 13, 15	Bancroft Library, University of California, Berkeley
63, 67	James Blank: San Diego Convention Bureau
46, 47T, 47B, 48, 49	Walt Disney Co.
90	Lee Foster
26B	Glynn Genin
52	Gondola Getaway
40	J Paul Getty Museum
39T, 39B	J Paul Getty Trust
18, 23, 59	Catherine Karnow
26T	Kal Kulter
31, 45, 76	Bret R Lundberg
60	Palm Springs Tourist Board
34	Carole Pearlman
79	Pollare/Fischer Communications
12	Seaver Center for Western History
Managing Editor	Martha Ellen Zenfell
Production Editor	Stuart A. Everitt
Cover Design	Klaus Geisler
Cartography	Berndtson & Berndtson

Burbank → Oakland.
Airport Shuttle. NOTES
S.F Airport.

1) Disneyland ~ car.   JS/MH
2) Catalina — Sat/Sun. AU
3) Universal — Fri AU
4) ~~Sea World~~
5) ~~Mexico~~
6) ~~Venta~~
7) ~~Sunset/Hollywood Sign/Park/~~
8) ~~Santa Monica Boulevard~~
9) Melrose Avenue / Beverly Centre /
   Century City. JS/MH/EB.

7) Hollywood / Stars / Hands /
   Re cho / Paramount.
8) Muscle Beach / Santa Monica JS/MH
   Venice .   ↗

4) Stars Home Tow.

6) Long Beach Cpina

CD Player. - Ben.

Dúras le Mr Candy gur bhaol liom go bhfliuchfaí go craiceann é ag dul abhaile. An freagra a thug sé orm, gurbh ionadh leis fear de m'aois, gan a bheith de thuiscint agam go raibh craiceann dochtúra do-fhliuchraiste. Agus d'imigh sé leis faoin mbáisteach, agus é ag gáire le neart an tsuilt a fuair sé ina ghreann féin; agus sin mar a scaramar le cuideachta na proinne.

———————

Imirt Chalaoiseach agus Garbhimirt:

(a) Áireofar ina chalaois aon tulcáil, cor coise, speachadh, breith, feidhm-choinneáil nó léim in aghaidh imreora; imreoir a bhac le lámh nó le géag cé ná feidhm-choinnítear é; nó síneadh de leith cúil imreora a bhíonn i seilbh na liathróide.

(b) Ní ceadaithe ruathar ó chúl a thabhairt faoi aon imreoir agus ní ceadaithe ruathar a thabhairt faoi aon imreoir ná cur isteach air in aon slí mura mbíonn sé ar tí an liathróid d'imirt nó le linn a himeartha dó. (Má thugann imreoir ruathar faoi imreoir eile a chasann d'aon toisc chun go dtiocfadh an ruathar, a bheadh cothrom mura mbeadh san, de leith a chúil, ní áireofar an ruathar sin ina chalaois.

(c) I gcás garbhimeartha, beidh ar an Réiteoir foláireamh a thabhairt don imreoir nó do na himreoirí agus má athchiontaítear amhlaidh beidh air an ciontóir nó na ciontóirí d'ordú ón réileán agus tuarascáil dá réir a chur chun an Choiste nó na Comhairle a bhíonn i gceannas an luaiteachais.

(d) I gcás imirt chontúirteach, foréigin, caint ghriogtha nó míchuí, nó i gcás imreoir a thógáil a láimhe chun bagirt ar imreoir eile nó chun é a bhualadh nó chun agartha, beidh ar an Réiteoir, gan aon fholáireamh, an ciontóir nó na ciontóirí a ordú den réileán agus tuarascáil dá réir a chur chun an Choiste nó na Comhairle a bhíonn i gceannas an luaiteachais.

Leaganacha Fraincise

Alt/Ráiteas le Jacques Poos, Aire Gnóthaí Eachtracha Lucsamburg, 1 Iúil 1997 (féach leathanaigh 150-151).

Les chefs d'État et de gouvernement réunis les 16 et 17 juin à Amsterdam ont donné à la présidence luxembourgeoise le mandat d'organiser un Conseil européen extraordinaire sur l'emploi. Ils ont ainsi voulu signaler qu'ils sont sensibles aux préoccupations des citoyens européens. Jamais, auparavant, une réunion d'un tel niveau ne s'était occupée directement et exclusivement du chômage, pourtant qualifié par tous de plus grand fléau de l'économie européenne...

Mais que peut faire l'Union sur la question de l'emploi?

Elle doit d'abord garantir un cadre macro-économique stable...

Il faudra ensuite moderniser les marchés du travail, stimuler au sein de l'UE l'échange d'informations sur les bonnes pratiques en matière d'emploi, soutenir la création et l'accès aux emplois de proximité, inciter différents organismes, comme la BEI, à investir dans le secteur des petites et moyennes entreprises, qui constitue le plus grand potentiel de création d'emplois en Europe...

L'investissement en Europe ne vise plus tant l'amélioration de la productivité des entreprises. Il se laisse tenter par les délocalistions vers les pays à bas salaire, voire par des restructurations globales qui ne font que peu de cas de la productivité atteinte dans les unités de production d'un grand groupe...

Les choses commencent cependant à bouger... Le terrain pour une réflexion, voire un dialogue plus global sur l'investissement en Europe et son lien avec le modèle social européen, existe donc... Les réflexions et suggestions des gouvernements et des partenaires sociaux pourraient devenir le sel du Sommet.

Conradh Maastricht, Airteagal 109j.1 (féach leathanaigh 152-153).

Les rapports examinent également si un degré élevé de convergence durable a été réalisé, en analysant dans quelle mesure chaque État membre a satisfait aux critères suivants:

- la réalisation d'un degré élevé de stabilité des prix; cela ressortira d'un taux d'inflation proche de celui des trois États membres, présentant les meilleurs résultats en matière de stabilité des prix;

- le caractère soutenable de la situation des finances publiques; cela ressortira d'une situation budgétaire qui n'accuse pas de déficit public excessif;

- le respect des marges normales de fluctuation prévues par le mécanism de change du système monétaire européen pendant deux ans au moins, sans dévaluation de la monnaie par rapport à celle d'un autre État membre;

Dracula, le Bram Stoker, caibidil VII, (féach leathanaigh 154-155).

Alors, sans aucun présage, la tempête éclata. Avec une rapidité qui paraissait, à ce moment, incroyable, et qui, même avec le recul, est impossible à comprendre, la nature entière parut se tordre. Les vagues naquirent, furieuses, comme jaillies du plus profond des mers, la suivante submergeant toujours la précédente - en quelques minutes, la mer d'huile s'était transformée en un monstre rugissant, affamé. Les vagues, couronnées de blanc, giflèrent avec furie les plages de sable et montèrent à l'assaut des falaises; d'autres se brisaient sur les quais et leur écume masquait parfois tout à fait le lueur des phares qui se dressent au bout de chacun des quais du port. Le vent hurlait comme le tonnerre, soufflait avec une force telle que les hommes les plus solides éprouvaient toutes les peines du monde à rester debout, et devaient s'agripper, de toute leur énergie, aux étais du port.

Caibidil 9
Foclóirí agus Foinsí eile Eolais

Leabharliosta deiridh

Foclóirí nach bhfuil luaite cheana

Foclóir Gaedhilge agus Béarla, Pádraig Ó Duinnín, BÁC, 1927.

Larger English-Irish Dictionary, O'Neill Lane, BÁC, 1918.

Foclóir Béarla agus Gaeilge/English-Irish Dictionary, Lambert Mac Cionnaith, BÁC, 1935.

Cnósach Focal ó Bhaile Bhúirne, Mícheál Ó Briain/Brian Ó Cuív, BÁC, 1947.

Liosta Focal as Ros Muc, T. S. Ó Máille, Preas Ollscoile Éireann, 1974

An Deascán Foclóireachta arna fhoilsiú ag Acadamh Ríoga na hÉireann, (ina bhfuil stórfhocail is 'leaganacha cainte nach bhfuil in FGB agus bríonna is struchtúir úsáide nach luaitear le focail atá in FGB')

1. *Innéacs Nua-Ghaeilge*, Tomás de Bhaldraithe, 1981. (Déanann sé an ceangal idir na ceannfhocail chaighdeánacha in FGB agus an leagan atá in DIL; an-úsáideach maidir le ceisteanna sanasaíochta.)

2. *Liosta Focal as Idir Shúgradh agus Dáiríre*, Séamus Ó Murchú, 1982.

3. *Díolaim Focal (A) ó Chorca Dhuibhne*, Éamonn Ó hÓgáin, 1984.

4. *Foirisiún Focal as Gaillimh*, Tomás de Bhaldraithe, 1985.

5. *Cnuasach Focal as Ros Goill*, Leaslaoi U. Lúcas, 1986.

6. *Cnuasach Focal ó Uíbh Ráthach*, Caoilfhionn Nic Pháidín, 1987.

7. *Díolaim Dhéiseach*, Diarmaid Ó hAirt, 1988.

8. *Cnuasach Focal as Teileann*, Úna M. Uí Bheirn, 1989.

Cnuasach Focal ón gCom, Daithí Ó Luineacháin, Coiscéim, 1995

Lexique Étymologique de l'Irlandais ancien, J. Vendryes, BÁC.

A.   1981
B.   (par les soins de E. Bachellery/P-Y. Lambert), 1981
C.   (par les soins de E. Bachellery/P-Y. Lambert), 1987
MNOP.   athchló, 1983.
RS.   (par les soins de E. Bachellery/P-Y. Lambert), 1974.
TU   (par les soins de E. Bachellery/P-Y. Lambert), 1978.

Collins Gem Irish Dictionary, Séamus Mac Mathúna/Ailbhe Ó Corráin, Londain, 1994.

Feic freisin na foclóirí éagsúla atá liostaithe faoi Noda i dtosach an leabhair seo.

Aguisín de théarmaí nach bhfuil lucht na Gaeilge ar aon aigne fúthu.

Focail/abairtí nach bhfuil socair nó nár mhiste don aistritheoir bheith an-chúramach ina n-úsáid:

balance: *cothromaíocht; comhardú, cóimheá, cothroime.*

complexity: FB, (of organism) *aimpléiseacht* (in FGB); TP, visual c., *meascra radhairc*; TCP, c. division/multiplication: *roinnt, iolrú coimpléascach* (*coimpléascúil*, in FF).

conditions: *dálaí fostaíochta* agus *coinníollacha fostaíochta.*

conversion: fraudulent conversion: *comhshó calaoiseach* in TD; in TR tá *tiontú* ach *trealamh tiontúcháin* (conversion equipment); in EBh tá *athchóiriú* (conversion of room); in TP tá *athchóiriú* (of building) agus *sóinseáil airgeadra* (currency conversion); in FCT tá *oiriúnú* (of timber) nó *tiontú*; in FEol tá *coinbhéartú* (mth)/*tiontú* (ph) agus *leictreon tiontaithe*, 'conversion electron', agus *fachtóir coinbhéartacha*, 'conversion factor'; in TTR, tá *scagaire cúitimh*, 'conversion filter'; in FT tá *comhshó bia*, 'food conversion'; in FSG tá *comhshó/comhshóiteacht* 'currency, debt conversion' agus *claochlú amhábhair*, 'conversion of

raw material' (*claochlú* = 'transmutation' in FEol, 'metamorphosis' in FT, 'transformation' in FC, TR, FB, agus tá *claonchló*, 'negative' in FGB, TTR); in FBith. tá *comhshó/athrú* agus *fachtóir comhshóch*, 'conversion factor'; ach tugtar *malartú, iompú, tiontú* in FS.

convertible: in FC, tá *cuntraphointe inchoinbhéartaithe* ar 'convertible counterpoint', ach in FSG, tá *insóinseáilte, inchomhshóite*, (os a choinne sin is *do-mhalairte* a thugtar ar 'inconvertible' cé go dtugtar *airgeadra do-chomhshóite* faoi 'inconvertible currency' agus in FF, *inchoinbhéartaithe*).

consideration: TP, planning, *cúrsaí le háireamh sa phleanáil*, strategy c., *tosca straitéise*; FSG, *comaoin*.

consistency: TCP, Mth, *comhsheasmhacht*; TR, *seiceáil chomhsheasmhachta* (consistency check); EBh, *raimhre, dlús*; FEol, *raimhre, téagar* (of substance) (consistence, Mth, *comhsheasmhacht*) ; FT, consistence (of horizon), *comhcháilíocht*; (FF, consistent, *comhsheasmhach*).

contamination: FEol, *éilliú, éilliúchán*; FT, *fabhtú, éilliú* (soil contamination: *fabhtú ithreach*; contaminated soil: *ithir fhabhtaithe*); TP, *éilliú* (of land: *éilliú talún*); EBh, FB, *fabhtú*; FS, *salú*.

convergence: FEol, Mth, *coinbhéirseacht*; FT, *coinbhéirseacht*; FR, *inréimneacht*; EID, *comhchlaontacht, comhchruinniú* (tugtar 'localization of industry' ar *comhchruinniú tionscal* in FGB agus tugtar 'concentration' air in FGB), *coinbhéirsiú*; in FGB tá *comhchlaonadh* agus is é *cóineasú* an focal a úsáidtear san Aontas Eorpach!

convergency: FEol. Mth, *coinbhéirseacht*; Ph. *inréimneacht*; FF, *inréimneacht*.

composition: FEol, FR, *comhshuíomh*; FT, *comhdhéanamh*; CH, *comhshuíomh*; TP, *comhshuíomh* (grassland composition: *comhshuíomh féarthailte*); FC, *cumadóireacht, comhdhéanamh séise*, composition of melody; FSG, sales c.: *comhdhéanamh díolachán*, fallacy of c, *fallás an chomhshuímh*, EBh, FB, *comhdhéanamh, comhshuíomh*; FCT, *comhshuíomh, comhdhéanamh, comhchumasc*; TTR, *comhdhéanamh*, musical c.: *saothar ceoil*; FS,

comhshuíomh bainne; FF, *comhchur*.

decomposition: FEol, FT, TP, FB, *dianscaoileadh*.

decontamination: FEol, *dí-éilliú, dí-éilliúchán*; FS, *díshalú*.

defect: FS, *éalang(ach)*,FSG, GTT, *locht(ach)*; FR, *fabht*; FF, *éalang, locht;* FB, *éalang (ó bhroinn)*, congenital defect; agus in FCT, tá *fabht, locht, máchail.* In TD tá *locht* ach *éalang teidil,* defect of title, agus tugtar *duine meabhairéalangach* ar 'mental defective'.

deficiency: FEol, *díothacht* (FGB, want, destitution; FS, deprivation: *díothacht oideachasúil, mhothúcháin* (emotional d.), *d. fhisiceach*, physical d.); FT, *easpa;* TP, *easnamh* (rainfall deficiency: *easnamh báistí*) also = deficit; FSG, *easnamh* (deficiency/payment account: *cuntas/íocaíocht easnaimh*) (also = deficit), agus in GTT,TR; EBh, *easnamh, díth* (vitamin deficiency, *díth vitimíní*); FB, *easpa, easpacht, díothacht* (demonstration of d. *taispeánadh easpachta/díothachta*; d. disease: *galar easpa*; ach in FT, *galar easpa*, agus *galar díothachta*); FS, *uireasa*, dietary d.: *uireasa cothaithe* (!!!), mental d.: *meabhairuireasa*, iodine d.: *uireasa iaidín*; FF, deficiency, *easnamh*.

deformation: FEol, Eng, *dífhoirmiú* (process), *dífhoirmíocht* (result), Mec Mth, *díchumadh* (deformation band: *banda díchumtha*!!!) (tugtar 'distortion' ar '*díchumadh*' in FR), TP, *míchumadh* (fós sa téacs) (> *dífhoirmiú*); FCT, *díchumadh* (elastic d. : *díchumadh leaisteach*); FS, *míchuma* (= deformation, deformity), congenital deformity: *míchuma chomhbheirthe.*

delinquency: TP, *ciontóireacht.*

dereliction: TP, FSG, *dearóiliú.*

disinfect: FT, FB, FS, *dífhabhtaigh* (also 'debugging' FSG,TR,TL); EBh, *dífhabhtaigh, díghalraigh.*

formation: FEol, Chem, *déanmhaíocht;* TP, *foirmíocht, foirmiú (foirmiú cladaigh* ach *foirmíocht charraige!*); FC, FSG, *foirmiú;* FB, FS, *foirmíocht, foirmiú;* TCP, *foirmíocht dromchla* (surface f.); FR, *foirmiú.*

foul = *calaois* (peil), níl sé in FGB ach tá sé in FP.

global: TP, *domhanda, gréasán* d. (global pattern); FEol. *cuimsitheach,* uile-; TR, *cuimsitheach.*

information: *faisnéis/eolas.*

institute: *institiúid/foras airgeadais.*

interdependence: *comhspleáchas* (TP), *idirspleáchas/ idirthuilleamaíocht* (FSG), níl ceachtar acu in FGB

integral response: FCT, *freagairt shuimeálach.*

integrate: TR, integrated, *iomlánaithe, comhtháite*; FR, *solas comhtháite.*

integrated database management system (TR): *córas bainistíochta bunachar sonraí comhtháite.*

integrated management information system (TR): *córas comhtháite eolais bhainistíochta.*

integration: FEol, Mth, *suimeáil*; (integrated, *iomlánaithe*); TP, *comhréimniú* (ciníocha), horizontal/vertical i., *comhréimniú cothrománach/ceartingearach, iomlánú draenála, lánpháirtiú polaitiúil, lánaontú* (of schools, factories); FSG, *imeascadh*, backward i., *cúlchumasc*, economic i. *lánpháirtíocht gheilleagrach*, forward i., *réamhlánpháirtiú*, horizontal/vertical i., *imeascadh cothrománach/ingearach: ceartingearach*, monetary i., *imeascadh airgeadaíochta*; FF, *iomlánú*, integrity: TR, *sláine.*

justify: *comhfhadaigh* (TR), *fírinnigh* (FGB).

performance management system (CT,8.4.97): *córas bainistíochta ar fheidhmiú.*

performance related pay (CT,8.4.97*): pá i gcoibhneas le feidhmiú.*

potential: feic EID, FSG (*poitéinseal margaidh* = market potential; potential demand = *éileamh féideartha*); FCT, Elec. *poitéinseal* (p. difference: *difríocht poitéinsil*); TTR, p. audience: *lucht éisteachta/féachana dóchúil*; FF, *tualangach.*

Read-only: compact disc read-only memory (TL*): dlúthdhiosca cuimhne léimh amháin.*

refractory: *teasfhulangach* (FEol, CH-PH); *easumhal, ceanndána* (EID); *casachtach - doleigheasta, ainsealach* (EID); FR, refraction, *athraonadh.*

rehabilitation (of land), *athinmheachán* (CT,10.1.94), (telecom) *athinmhiú* (CT,88); *athshlánú* (TP); *athshlánú*, *athinmheachán* (FS).

rejuvenation: *feabhsú* (FT).

repercussion: *frithbhualadh* (pléascán); *frithiarmhairt* (FSG).

replacement: FEol, Geol, *athsholáthar*, CH, *cur in ionad*; TP, r. cost, *costas athsholáthair* (FSG), r. deposit, *sil-leagan ionaid*, r. ores, *mianta ionaid*; FSG, replacement investment/price, *infheistíocht/praghas athsholáthair*; TTR, (audio) dialogue replacement: *aisghuthú*; TL r. copy: *athchóip*.

resistance: *friotaíocht*; fire resistance: *dó-obacht*; resistance fighter: *trodaire frithbheartaíochta*.

responsive: EID - they are responsive to affection: *ceannsaíonn an chineáltacht iad*; ach labour markets responsive to economic change: *? inoiriúnaithe, inchurtha in oiriúint* (EID).

restoration: (of land) *athchóiriú* (CT,10.1.94), *athshlánaigh* (FSG); *athchóiriú, athdheisiú* (FCT); *athchóiriú* (TP, FT); níl aon téarma in TL a bhainfeadh le leabhair.

tactics: tugtar *beartaíocht* in EID agus in *Liosta de Théarmaí Staire* (gan dáta) ach tá *oirbheartaíocht* in FSG; déanann FGB an t-idirdhealú: *beartaíocht* = scheming, ingenuity, ach is ionann *oirbheartaíocht* agus 'tactics' (mil.); ach níl aon aidiacht ann: *pleanáil oirbheartaíochta* (tactical planning) atá in FSG, agus *taiscéalaíocht oirbheartaíochta* (tactical reconnaisance) in FGB; tugann EID *beartach* air ach ní thugann FGB 'tactical' mar mhíniú le *oirbheartach* ach practised, dexterous etc, nó b'fhéidir gurb ionann an chiall atá le 'skilful' nó 'ingenious' agus le 'tactical' de ghnáth. (Léiríonn an iontráil seo in FGB ceann de mhórdheacrachtaí na Gaeilge: tugtar 'infiltration tactics' ar *oirbheartaíocht insíothlaithe*, nuair nach gá gur ceann gníomhach atá ann ach a mhalairt.)